Better Homes and Gardens®

Best Buffets
Cook Book

Contents

On the cover: This happy threesome is enjoying a buffet featuring sliced ham, *Oven-Easy Barbecued Chicken,* fluffy *Orange-Chestnut Rice, Hot Vegetable Platter,* and a tossed salad (see menu, page 32).

BETTER HOMES AND GARDENS BOOKS

Editorial Director: Don Dooley
Managing Editor: Malcolm E. Robinson   Art Director: John Berg
Asst. Managing Editor: Lawrence D. Clayton   Asst. Art Director: Randall Yontz
Food Editor: Nancy Morton
Senior Food Editor: Joyce Trollope
Associate Editors: Rosemary Corsiglia, Sharyl Heiken
Assistant Editors: Sandra Mapes, Catherine Penney, Elizabeth Strait, Elizabeth Walter
Designer: Harijs Priekulis
Contributing Editor: Lorene Frohling

Our seal assures you that every recipe in *Best Buffets Cook Book* is endorsed by the Better Homes and Gardens Test Kitchen. Each recipe is tested for family appeal, practicality, and deliciousness.

Buffets for Casual Living

Do you often find mealtime a hectic experience that keeps you hopping from table to kitchen? If so, it's time you took advantage of the ease and flexibility of serving buffets— a simple way to adapt today's informal life-style to mealtime.

To get you started, use the next few pages as a primer for learning how to make your buffet meals a success. Note the suggestions for planning the buffet, varying the site, choosing table appointments, setting the table, and keeping all foods at the correct serving temperature.

Whether it's a friendly get-together or an everyday family meal, you'll appreciate knowing how to plan and serve buffets that let you relax and enjoy the meal with others.

A slim console table gives easy access to this Make-Ahead Buffet (see page 39). *Buffet Beef Rolls* are accompanied by *Potato-Mushroom Bake* and *Marinated Asparagus Salad.* Diners select dessert from the bowl of fresh fruit.

Easy Buffet Know-How

Successful buffets—whether large or small, simple or elaborate—have two features in common. First, the menu, serving line, and equipment combine to make good food easy to eat. Secondly, preparations, serving, and cleanup are easy for the homemaker to manage without extra help. The result is delicious food served in comfortable surroundings and enjoyed by diner and hostess alike.

With all this going for it, it's no wonder that a buffet is so right for the casual atmosphere of today's informal entertaining and family-centered activities. So, whether you're a novice, a recent convert, or a dedicated buffet buff, this emphasis on convenience in preparation and serving will help you turn your time, budget, living space, and equipment into the tasty menu and appropriate setting for a delightful meal.

Accomplishing this is not difficult, but it does take planning since the details are interrelated. However, if you tackle them one at a time, everything will work together and you won't overlook something that could keep your buffet from going smoothly.

Planning the Menu

Your time: Since buffets are do-it-yourself projects for the homemaker, plan a menu that you can conveniently do in the kind of time you have available. There's little point in a guest list of 20 if you haven't the time to prepare your buffet party for more than 10. Also, if you work during the day, you'll want to choose foods that can be made ahead, or else schedule the buffet for a weekend when you have more time to prepare for it. In any case, if you dovetail preparations so that there is a minimum to do at the last minute, you'll find you have a few moments to relax before the guests arrive.

Buffet foods: Although a buffet can be a smorgasbord with many food choices, it usually is not. Instead, a main dish, one or two vegetables, a salad, bread, dessert, and beverage are presented attractively from a central location. The variety of foods could change with the number on the guest list, but often it is easier to choose recipes that can be doubled or halved so you can keep the original menu plan intact. If you are leary of doubling a particular recipe, make two separate batches. As you page through this book, you'll note that many of the menus can be doubled or halved. Any special directions that are needed appear at the end of designated recipes, too.

Most foods are suitable for buffet service if you stick to the original guidelines of presenting good food that is easy to eat. But, if guests are expected to balance trays on their laps, avoid foods that require cutting. In fact, you can further eliminate the need for knives if you butter the bread before serving. If, however, guests will sit at tables after filling their plates, food requiring knives is appropriate.

Because all foods are picked up at the buffet table on one plate, it's wise to avoid overly saucy dishes. Likewise, don't serve foods such as baked soufflés, which have a very delicate structure and should be eaten immediately after baking. You don't want to hurry guests through the line before the soufflé falls. Besides, it's too much of a strain on your time schedule to have to work a soufflé into the meal.

Throughout this book, you'll find many menus and recipes to fit a wide variety of buffet serving situations. There are certain to be several that you can readily incorporate into your own plans.

Budget: The amount of money you want to spend also influences your final menu decision. Fortunately, buffets make friendly get-togethers possible on many occasions when the bank account prohibits some of the more ambitious types of entertaining.

Remember that a buffet doesn't have to involve a complete dinner from appetizer to dessert. It may consist of only a few appetizers, snacks, or light refreshments for friends or neighbors to enjoy at an open house or before a night on the town. At other times, plan the buffet around a glamorous dessert for couples after an evening of bridge. Likewise, a soup buffet served by the fire welcomes skiers and skaters.

The expense of dinner for a large group is easy to keep within bounds if you ask friends to bring a dish for a potluck buffet. The table fills quickly with an array of main dishes, salads, breads, and desserts with a minimum of expense to each participant. However, the potluck does require special planning to coordinate the menu and to make sure the costs are distributed equitably.

Theme: Not every buffet has to have a special party theme, but a theme can add to the fun and give you ideas for a centerpiece or other decorations. Often, the theme comes from a special cause for celebrating such as a birthday, anniversary, graduation, promotion, retirement, or vacation. And don't overlook national holidays, the change in seasons, or a local event as your inspiration. A touch of ingenuity will turn a humdrum day into a festive occasion.

How far you want to go with decorations depends on the occasion. If you are clever with scissors, you may want to design your own decorations. If you are not so handy, there is a wide assortment of ready-made favors and decorations available.

When a theme is planned, try to coordinate the menu with it, too. Greek, German, Mexican, or Oriental motifs call for foods representative of the individual country. Be careful about colors though. Red, white, and blue are fine for table decorations, but few blue foods are appetizing.

Using Space to Advantage

Determining size: Buffets come in all sizes. You don't need a baronial hall and a guest list of hundreds to capitalize on this versatile method of serving. In fact, buffet service is every bit as appropriate for four as 14 or 40. However, regardless of size, a realistic approach to the number of people who can congregate and eat comfortably in the space you have to use can spell the difference between enjoying the buffet and having a miserable time.

How large a party you can manage depends not so much on whether you live in a house or apartment as on how you utilize the space. After all, when food is served buffet-style, guests can move from room to room once they have filled their plates. Thus, chairs and small tables can be distributed through as many areas—living room, dining room, kitchen, patio, or deck—as you need. This mobility expands the usable space considerably.

Another way to handle the space problem is to stagger the arrival times on invitations so that people are coming and going throughout an extended serving period. This technique is particularly useful for either a formal tea or an informal open house.

Small parties need space planning, too. Just as important as having enough room is not having too much. Four or five guests wandering around your apartment or house limits the comradery. So, to control this, close off one or two rooms and limit your party area to comfortably accommodate the number of guests you invite.

Once you've established the outer limits of the party area, it is easy to determine the number of guests to invite and to plan where the serving areas will be.

Serving locations: Different types of buffets call for different settings. Don't resign yourself to serving all your buffets from the same spot. Even though you may have a space problem, chances are that a few minor furniture adjustments can make possible a multitude of new buffet table sites.

If you are lucky enough to have a long sideboard or a large-size dining table, you can centralize the buffet in a single area. Otherwise you'll probably need to divide the foods into smaller groupings. Use a tea cart or small table for the beverage. And serve the dessert from a small table, or clear the original buffet before presenting the dessert later.

If you like the idea of serving the buffet in courses, start out by letting friends help themselves to appetizers from the coffee table in the living room. Later, steer the party to a salad bar arranged on the kitchen counter. Then, use the dining table for serving the entrée and its accompaniments. And after the meal, set the dessert on a desk or game table in the family room.

There's no limit to the number of buffet sites you can discover around your own home. Stack the books in a closet while you serve from one or more shelves of a bookcase. Or, cover the top of a stereo or a baby grand piano with fabric and padding to protect the surfaces before setting out nibble foods or dips. Once you get going, you probably can think of many more usable locations.

Most of the buffets discussed so far are company meals, but you can liven up the everyday mealtime routine by summoning the family to a spread in the family room. Centralize the food on a coffee table, desk, or Ping-Pong table. If you're blessed with a fireplace, set the buffet on a low table nearby for a cozy family supper.

Many kitchens can accommodate an occasional breakfast or lunch buffet for the family. If it's a sleep-in morning, let straggling family members cook their own pancakes or waffles at a buffet brunch set on the kitchen counter. Or, reduce confusion of noon hours that don't coincide by serving lunch from a snack bar or work island in the kitchen.

Choosing the Appointments

A carefully planned buffet loses its pizzazz if the table looks jumbled and unattractive. Coordinating the table covering, dinnerware, glassware, flatware, serving pieces, and decorations need not be expensive or difficult.

First of all, decide the degree of formality or informality of the buffet. A quick inventory of the table appointments you have will influence the decision. If you don't have what you need for a large group, consider renting some pieces.

Table coverings and napkins: The amount of pattern and color needed in the cloth and napkins is largely dependent on the menu and on the design of the dinnerware. Too much pattern creates an unorganized feeling. Too little pattern produces a table setting that is dull or has an unfinished look.

Rather than purchasing a special cloth for the table, try using a handsome quilt, a large terry cloth beach towel, or a gaily colored sheet. Table coverings such as these make great conversation pieces.

Tables with self-protective finishes are ideal if you are using place mats or table runners. Make your own mats or runners, or select ready-made ones, which are available in a wide variety of shapes, colors, and sizes.

Napkins may match the table covering or provide a contrast to the setting. For very casual and informal buffets, use paper napkins or fingertip terry cloth towels.

Dinnerware and glassware: These items are not only essential to any buffet but they need to be both attractive and appropriate to the occasion. Earthenware, stoneware, pottery, glass, glass-ceramic, plastic, and paper plates lend an informal note to the table. Likewise,

One-line buffet

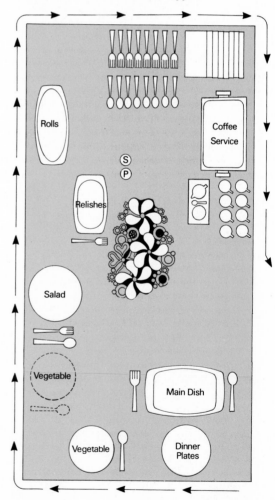

mugs, low or unfooted glasses, and plastic or paper cups set a casual tone. For a formal buffet, fine china and stemmed crystal generally are used.

Don't worry if you're short on matching place settings. As long as different patterns are compatible, you can mix them.

Flatware and serving pieces: Knives, forks, and spoons also must be coordinated with the mood of the buffet. Reserve ornate patterns in flatware for formal occasions, and use simpler patterns for informal settings. Plastic utensils are fine for most outdoor buffets.

Pitchers, trays, and other serving containers are available in sterling or plated silver, stainless steel, pewter, copper, and brass. The warm, cheery atmosphere of many casual buffets is sparked by an interesting brass tray, a handsome pewter pitcher, or a much-used antique copper teakettle.

Table decorations: Make the buffet centerpiece reflect the theme or mood of the party. Although a made-to-order arrangement is nice, it is frequently expensive. So, if you've budgeted your money elsewhere, create your own centerpiece. Since guests are never

Two-line buffet

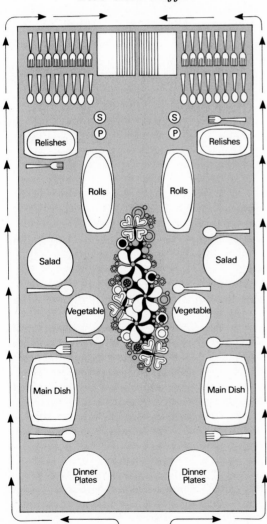

Buffet with beverage cart

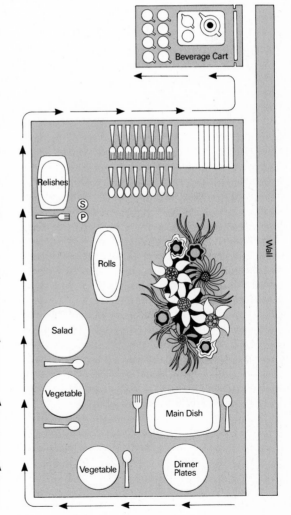

seated at a buffet table, the centerpiece can be more lavish and taller than would be practical at a sit-down dinner.

For starters, use fresh-cut flowers from the garden, or gather a bouquet of wild flowers from wooded areas. Fall is an excellent time of the year to stock up on interesting plants growing along the roadways. Combine these with wheat, milo heads, Indian corn, and gourds for a back-to-nature centerpiece. Many of these are reusable.

If you're fond of plants, chances are you have several attractive centerpieces on hand all the time. Or, if you're a collector of antique bowls, fill your favorite with a colorful arrangement of fresh vegetables or fruit. And don't forget that a decorated birthday cake or a fresh fruit plate can serve both as a centerpiece and dessert.

Candles also create an interesting mood used alone or in combination with the centerpiece. If tables are set for eating, put a lighted candle on each table to add interest. (Be sure that candle flames are not too close to plastic or paper items.)

Setting the Table

Unless you've had a lot of experience organizing buffets, it's a good idea to arrange all the serving dishes on the table in advance to make sure the surface is large enough, yet not too large. An undersized table crowds the platters and serving pieces and is an invitation to accidents; an oversized table makes the food appear skimpy.

Meal buffets: Whether you plan a one-line or a two-line buffet depends on the number of guests invited and the size of the room. Nothing is more frustrating to hungry friends than being at the end of a snail-paced buffet line. So, if space permits and you have two sets of serving dishes, organize the table in a two-line buffet.

Common sense dictates the order in which food is placed on the table. If trays are provided, place them at the beginning of the buffet either on the corner of the table or on a small table next to the buffet. (Note the diagrams on pages 8 and 9 for placement of food.) Allow plenty of room beside each

serving dish so that your guests can set down their trays or plates while they serve themselves. So that no one will have to juggle extra equipment as they move along, arrange flatware and napkins at the end of the line.

Depending on the eating arrangement, you may let guests select a beverage from a cart or small table placed at the end of the buffet. Or, you may pour the beverage at individual tables after your friends are seated. Often, it is more convenient to have eating tables set with flatware, napkins, and beverage so guests need only carry their plates from the buffet.

Tea buffets: Setting a buffet for a tea follows much the same pattern as a dinner buffet. A two-line buffet works best for large groups or for a reception that offers more than one beverage. (Note the diagrams on page 11.)

Set the buffet so that friends can pick up the beverage after filling their plates. This helps reduce the possibility of accidental spills. If coffee, tea, and punch are served, arrange the coffee and tea at one end and the punch at the opposite end. Direct guests to either side, depending on their choice of beverage.

Serving the Food

All the time spent in planning the buffet is of little use if hot foods have cooled and cold foods have warmed by the time guests reach the buffet. So, plan ahead to make sure foods are kept at the proper temperature on the buffet.

For large buffets, you may need to refill serving dishes or have one or more duplicate serving dishes to replace those on the table. Duplicate serving dishes often solve the temperature problem, as you can either keep them warm in the oven or cold in the refrigerator. If you use this system, be sure to watch the table and replace or refill dishes before they are completely empty.

Cold foods: Make certain that foods are thoroughly chilled before placing them on the buffet. Foods stay cold longer if they are chilled in the actual serving dish or if an insulated server is used. Some foods, such as cooked shrimp, melon wedges, and crisp relishes, are attractive and stay chilled when served in a bed of chipped ice. You can create your own icer for serving cold soups or fruit mixtures by setting the filled serving dish inside a large bowl or an ice bucket filled with chipped ice.

Molded salads generally stay firm if they are placed on the buffet just before serving time. If the weather is quite warm or if the salad will have to stand a long time, you can make the mold firmer by slightly reducing the amount of liquid in the recipe.

Hot foods: You don't have to invest money in extra equipment to keep food hot on the buffet. An inexpensive candle warmer is usually enough for keeping casseroles hot. Another thrifty idea is to cook and serve in the same appliance. The pretty designs of modern-day appliances make them appropriate buffet servers. Another example, the fondue pot, is ideal for keeping soups, gravies,

and creamed mixtures warm on the buffet. Be sure to set hot foods and warmers on trays, trivets, or pads to protect tabletops.

If you have a microwave oven, use it to quickly reheat food that has cooled. Another means of keeping foods hot on the buffet is to make use of special appliances, such as warming trays, pizza warmers, bun warmers, serving carts with a heated tray, electric hot plates, electric griddles, automatic hot pots, and electric or canned heat chafing dishes. If you plan to use an electric server make certain the buffet site is located near an electrical outlet. As a safety precaution, avoid letting the cord cross the traffic pattern around the buffet table.

Two-line tea buffet

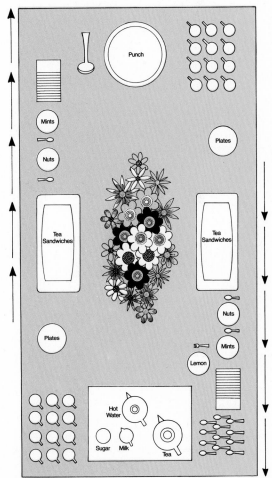

One-line tea buffet

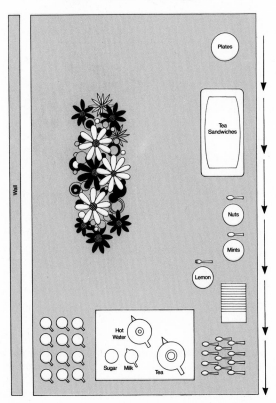

Buffets for Entertaining

Are you reluctant to invite a group of friends to a buffet because you are unsure what foods go well together for this help-yourself way of serving? For formal or informal buffets, there's no need to despair— if you just follow the menus and serving tips outlined here.

Whether your party numbers 4 or 24, you'll find ideas for serving a buffet brunch, lunch, dinner, or late-night supper. You'll also find help for halving or doubling some of the menus to fit the size of the group.

Don't hesitate to adapt the menus, themes, and serving suggestions to the space and equipment you have available. No doubt you'll soon be creating your own buffets from beginning to end and enjoying it.

Salmon-Crab Veronique is the chafing dish entrée for this elegant Seafood Buffet (see page 44). Guests spoon the luscious mixture over patty shells before helping themselves to *Lemon Broccoli* and *Mushroom-Spinach Toss*.

Brunches and Lunches

Patio Brunch
Serves 10

Bloody Mary Cocktails
Scrambled Eggs Deluxe
Ham Steaks
Golden Coffee Cake
Melon Buffet Bowl
Coffee

BUFFET SERVING TIP: A little planning keeps buffet foods at their best when brunch moves outdoors. Use an insulated ice bucket to keep fruit chilled and a chafing dish over hot water (bain-marie) to keep scrambled eggs warm. Grill ham on a tabletop griddle and place the coffee server on a warmer.

Scrambled Eggs Deluxe

20 eggs
1 cup light cream
½ teaspoon salt
¼ teaspoon pepper
1 cup shredded Swiss cheese
1 cup shredded sharp American cheese (4 ounces)
1 6-ounce can sliced mushrooms, drained
¼ cup butter or margarine
2 tablespoons snipped chives

In large mixing bowl beat together eggs, cream, salt, and pepper just till blended; stir in cheeses and mushrooms. In 12-inch skillet melt butter or margarine; add egg mixture. Cook, gently stirring and folding eggs; work from center to outside. Cook and fold till eggs are fully cooked, but still moist and glossy. Transfer to chafing dish. Garnish with snipped chives. Makes 10 servings.

Golden Coffee Cake

1 12-ounce can apricot nectar (1½ cups)
1 13¾-ounce package hot roll mix
½ cup butter or margarine, melted
2 slightly beaten eggs
2 tablespoons sugar
½ cup dried currants
½ teaspoon rum extract
½ cup apricot preserves

Warm ¾ *cup* nectar (110°); add yeast from hot roll mix. Stir to dissolve yeast. Add butter, eggs, sugar, and flour from hot roll mix; beat smooth. Stir in currants; turn into greased 9-inch fluted tube pan or 2-quart ring mold. Let dough rise till double (1 to 1½ hours). Bake at 350° for 35 to 40 minutes. Heat ⅔ *cup* of the nectar with extract. With long skewer or 2-tined fork make punctures 2 inches deep at close intervals in top of warm cake. Pour hot nectar mixture over. Let stand 15 minutes. Invert on cooling rack placed over paper. Heat preserves with remaining nectar; spoon over cake. Serve cooled or chilled. Makes 1.

Melon Buffet Bowl

Combine ½ cup light corn syrup, ¼ cup orange liqueur, and ¼ cup bottled sweetened lime juice. Pour syrup mixture over mixture of 3 cups honeydew melon balls; 3 cups pineapple chunks; 3 medium oranges, peeled and sectioned; and 2 cups green or red grapes, halved and seeded. Cover. Chill several hours or overnight; stir gently once or twice. Garnish with fresh mint. Serves 10.

A day-brightening menu

Brunch in a shady corner of the patio features a →
colorful *Melon Buffet Bowl,* fluffy *Scrambled Eggs Deluxe,* ham, and *Golden Coffee Cake.* Start the meal with Bloody Mary cocktails, if desired.

Guest Brunch

Serves 6

Orange Juice
Granola   Light Cream
Sausage Brunch Cake
Baked Eggs
Cantaloupe Pleaser
Milk   Coffee

BUFFET SERVING TIP: Plan a fall theme to accent the colors in this menu. Center the buffet with an arrangement of wheat or milo heads, cattails, acorns, and colorful fall leaves. Use wooden accessories and remember to provide trays for carrying food from the buffet to the eating area.

Granola

Serve this nutritious cereal mixture with cream or eat it plain as a snack—

　　6 cups rolled oats
　　1 cup shredded coconut
　　1 cup wheat germ
　　¾ cup cashew nuts, halved
　　½ cup shelled sunflower seeds
　　　• • •
　　½ cup cooking oil
　　½ cup honey
　　⅓ cup water
　　1½ teaspoons salt
　　1½ teaspoons vanilla
　　1 cup raisins

In large bowl combine rolled oats, shredded coconut, wheat germ, cashew nuts, and sunflower seeds. Mix together cooking oil, honey, water, salt, and vanilla; pour over oatmeal mixture. Stir well to coat.

Spread cereal mixture on two greased baking sheets. Bake at 350° for 30 minutes, stirring cereal mixture frequently; cool thoroughly. Stir in raisins. Store cereal mixture in an airtight container till ready to serve. Makes about 11 cups cereal.

Sausage Brunch Cake

　　1 8-ounce package brown-and-serve
　　　sausage links
　　3 tablespoons butter or margarine
　　3 tablespoons orange marmalade
　　1 14-ounce package apple-cinnamon
　　　muffin mix

In skillet brown the sausage according to package directions; drain. In 9x9x2-inch baking pan melt butter; stir in marmalade. Arrange sausage in two rows atop marmalade mixture. Prepare muffin mix according to package directions; spoon batter atop sausage. Bake at 350° till golden brown, 30 to 35 minutes. Immediately invert on serving platter. Makes 1 coffee cake.

Baked Eggs

　　6 eggs
　　6 teaspoons milk

Butter 6 custard cups. Break *one* egg into each cup; sprinkle with a little salt and pepper. To each egg add *1 teaspoon* of the milk. Set custard cups in shallow baking pan; pour hot water into pan to depth of 1 inch. Bake at 350° till eggs are set, about 25 minutes. Makes 6 servings.

Cantaloupe Pleaser

　　¼ cup sugar
　　3 tablespoons lime juice
　　2 cups cantaloupe balls
　　2 nectarines, pitted and sliced
　　1 7-ounce bottle ginger ale, chilled
　　　Fresh mint sprigs

Combine sugar and lime juice; stir till sugar dissolves. Pour lime mixture over cantaloupe and nectarines in deep bowl; stir gently to coat fruit. Cover and chill thoroughly, stirring once or twice.

To serve, place fruit mixture in glass serving bowl or spoon into individual sherbet glasses; carefully pour ginger ale over fruit. Garnish with mint. Makes 6 servings.

Saturday Brunch
Serves 8 (halve for 4)

Fruit Compote
Crisp-Cooked Bacon
Pumpkin Puff Pancakes
Butter   Hot Cider Sauce
Cranberry Syrup
Maple-Orange Syrup
Milk   Coffee

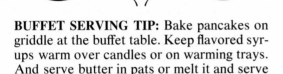

BUFFET SERVING TIP: Bake pancakes on griddle at the buffet table. Keep flavored syrups warm over candles or on warming trays. And serve butter in pats or melt it and serve in a small pitcher for guests to pour over hot pancakes at the serving table.

Pumpkin Puff Pancakes
Offer a choice of flavored syrups with these light, feathery cakes—

2 cups all-purpose flour
2 tablespoons sugar
4 teaspoons baking powder
1 teaspoon salt
1 teaspoon ground cinnamon
• • •
2 cups milk
1 cup canned pumpkin
4 slightly beaten egg yolks
¼ cup butter or margarine, melted
4 stiffly beaten egg whites

In large mixing bowl thoroughly stir together the flour, sugar, baking powder, salt, and cinnamon. Combine milk, pumpkin, beaten egg yolks, and melted butter or margarine. Add milk mixture to dry ingredients, stirring just till dry ingredients are moistened. Fold in stiffly beaten egg whites.

Using about ⅓ *cup* pancake batter for each pancake, bake on hot, lightly greased griddle, turning once. Serve pancakes with Hot Cider Sauce, Cranberry Syrup, and Maple-Orange Syrup. Makes 16 pancakes.

Fruit Compote

Combine two 10-ounce packages frozen strawberries, thawed; 2 medium bananas, sliced; 2 oranges, peeled and sectioned; and ½ teaspoon ground cinnamon. Chill overnight. Makes 8 servings.

Hot Cider Sauce

¾ cup apple juice *or* apple cider
½ cup packed brown sugar
½ cup light corn syrup
2 tablespoons butter or margarine
½ teaspoon lemon juice
⅛ teaspoon ground cinnamon
⅛ teaspoon ground nutmeg

Combine all ingredients; bring to a boil. Simmer 15 minutes. Makes 1¼ cups.

Cranberry Syrup

¾ cup packed brown sugar
¾ cup water
¼ cup maple-flavored syrup
2 cups cranberries
2 tablespoons butter or margarine

In medium saucepan combine brown sugar, water, and syrup; stir to dissolve sugar. Heat to boiling; reduce heat. Simmer, uncovered, for 5 minutes. Add cranberries; cook till skins pop, about 5 minutes. Remove from heat; press through sieve or food mill. Stir in butter. Serve warm. Makes 1¾ cups.

Maple-Orange Syrup

1 6-ounce can frozen orange juice
   concentrate
⅔ cup maple-flavored syrup
⅓ cup packed brown sugar
⅓ cup water
2 tablespoons butter or margarine

Combine all ingredients. Bring to a boil; reduce heat. Simmer 10 minutes, stirring occasionally. Serve warm. Makes about 1¾ cups.

Western Brunch
Serves 8

Salt Lick Pitcher
Gold Rush Brunch
Apple-Spice Nuggets
Raspberry-Orange Cups
Milk   Coffee

BUFFET SERVING TIP: For a Western atmosphere, place the food on a buffet table made of rough board planks set on sawhorses. Use casual pottery or stoneware and bandanna napkins. Complete the theme with a centerpiece of cacti and succulents.

Gold Rush Brunch

    1 5½-ounce package dry hashed brown
        potatoes with onion
    ¼ cup butter or margarine
    ¼ cup all-purpose flour
    ½ teaspoon salt
    ⅛ teaspoon pepper
    2 cups milk
    1 cup dairy sour cream
    2 tablespoons snipped parsley
    8 slices Canadian-style bacon,
        cut ¼ inch thick
    8 eggs

Prepare potatoes according to package directions; set aside. In 3-quart saucepan melt butter; blend in flour, salt, and pepper. Add milk all at once; cook and stir till thickened and bubbly. Remove from heat. Stir in sour cream, parsley, and hashbrowns. Turn into 13x9x2-inch baking dish. Arrange Canadian-style bacon in a row down center, overlapping slices slightly. Bake, uncovered, at 350° for 20 minutes.

   Remove from oven. Make 4 depressions on each side of bacon; slip *one* egg into each depression. Sprinkle with salt and pepper. Return to oven; bake till eggs are set, 10 to 12 minutes longer. Serves 8.

Salt Lick Pitcher

In a large pitcher combine 2 cups vodka (16 ounces); 2 cups grapefruit juice, chilled; and two 7-ounce bottles *or* 2 cups tonic water, chilled. Moisten the rims of eight 8-ounce glasses with lemon juice; then swirl in salt to form a frosted ring around the glasses. Pour vodka mixture into the glasses and fill with ice cubes. Garnish with maraschino cherries, if desired. Serves 8.

Apple-Spice Nuggets

    1½ cups all-purpose flour
    ½ cup sugar
    2 teaspoons baking powder
    ½ teaspoon salt
    ½ teaspoon ground cinnamon
    ¼ teaspoon ground nutmeg
    ¾ cup shredded peeled apple
    1 well-beaten egg
    ⅓ cup cooking oil
    ¼ cup milk
            • • •
    ½ cup butter or margarine, melted
    ¾ cup sugar
    1 teaspoon ground cinnamon
    1 teaspoon ground nutmeg

Thoroughly stir together first 6 ingredients; stir in apple. Combine egg, oil, and milk. Add all at once to flour mixture; stir just till dry ingredients are moistened. Fill greased 1¾-inch miniature muffin pans ⅔ full. Bake at 350° about 20 minutes. Dip hot muffins in butter; shake gently in plastic bag with mixture of ¾ cup sugar, 1 teaspoon cinnamon, and 1 teaspoon nutmeg. Makes 32.

Raspberry-Orange Cups

Remove tops of 8 medium oranges. With grapefruit knife scoop out and dice pulp. Reserve orange shells. Combine pulp, 2 tablespoons powdered sugar, and 2 tablespoons brandy; toss gently with 2 cups raspberries. Spoon fruit mixture into orange shells. Chill. Before serving, sprinkle additional powdered sugar atop each serving. Serves 8.

Weekend Brunch

Serves 12 (halve for 6)

Chilled Tangerine Juice
Brunch Egg Bake
Toasted English Muffins
Sweet Cinnamon Drops
Fresh Fruit Kabobs
Milk   Coffee

BUFFET SERVING TIP: Doubling the guest list doesn't have to double the work load. Use colorful paper plates to brighten the table and to lighten the work; provide wicker liners for sturdiness. For an unusual centerpiece, spear fruit kabobs into whole pineapples. Keep juice chilled in an ice bucket and let guests help themselves.

Fresh Fruit Kabobs

Orange liqueur sparks the marinade for these tasty kabobs. Vary the fruit with the season—

  ½ cup sugar
  ¼ cup lemon juice
  ¼ cup water
  3 tablespoons orange liqueur
     • • •
  4 medium nectarines *or* peaches
  ½ medium pineapple
  1 pint whole strawberries, chilled

Combine sugar, lemon juice, water, and orange liqueur in shallow dish. If using peaches, peel. Pit nectarines or peaches; cut into wedges. Add to liqueur mixture; stir to coat cut surfaces of fruit. Peel, remove eyes, and core pineapple; cut into bite-size cubes. Add to marinade; stir gently. Cover and refrigerate overnight; stir occasionally. Before serving, drain nectarines and pineapple, reserving marinade. Thread nectarine wedges and pineapple cubes on appetizer skewers with chilled whole strawberries. Drizzle reserved marinade over all fruits on skewers. Makes 12 servings.

Brunch Egg Bake

Eggs bake in a cheesy sauce—

  8 slices bacon
  3 cups chopped onion
  2 10½-ounce cans condensed cream of
     chicken soup
  1 cup milk
  1 teaspoon prepared mustard
  1½ cups shredded sharp American
     cheese (6 ounces)
  12 eggs
     • • •
  6 English muffins, split, toasted, and
     buttered

In skillet cook bacon till crisp; drain, reserving ¼ cup bacon drippings. Crumble bacon; set aside. In same skillet cook chopped onion in reserved drippings till tender. Add condensed cream of chicken soup, milk, and prepared mustard; cook, stirring constantly, till mixture is smooth and heated through. Add shredded sharp American cheese and stir till the cheese is melted.

Pour *1 cup* of the sauce into each of two 10x6x2-inch baking dishes. Break 6 eggs into sauce in each baking dish; carefully spoon *half* of remaining sauce around eggs in each baking dish. Sprinkle *half* of the bacon atop each casserole. Bake at 350° till eggs are set, about 20 minutes.

To serve, spoon eggs and sauce atop buttered muffin halves. Makes 12 servings.
To serve 6: Use half recipe and bake in individual casseroles till eggs are set.

Sweet Cinnamon Drops

  2 cups packaged biscuit mix
  ⅔ cup water
  ¼ cup sugar
  1 teaspoon ground cinnamon

In mixing bowl combine biscuit mix, water, and *half* of the sugar till well blended. Drop dough from teaspoon into mixture of remaining sugar and cinnamon. Roll each ball to coat entire surface. Place on greased baking sheet. Bake at 350° till golden brown, 10 to 12 minutes. Makes 24 rolls.

Slim Ham Slaw served in a hollowed-out cabbage shell makes an eye-catching centerpiece for the buffet table, as well as an appealing and satisfying main dish salad for your calorie-counting guests.

Tomato Cocktail

    3 cups tomato juice
    2 tablespoons lemon juice
    1 tablespoon chopped celery leaves
    ¼ teaspoon onion powder
    1 bay leaf
      Several drops bottled hot pepper
        sauce
      Lemon wedges

In saucepan combine tomato juice, lemon juice, chopped celery leaves, onion powder, bay leaf, and hot pepper sauce. Heat mixture to boiling; reduce heat and simmer 10 minutes. Remove from heat; cover and chill 6 hours or overnight. Strain.

    Serve chilled juice in appetizer glasses; garnish each glass with a lemon wedge. Makes 6 servings. (21 calories/serving.)

Yogurt Topping

    1 tablespoon sugar
    2 teaspoons cornstarch
    ½ teaspoon shredded orange peel
    ⅔ cup orange juice
    ⅓ cup plain yogurt
    ⅓ cup frozen whipped dessert topping,
        thawed
      Fresh fruit

In saucepan combine sugar and cornstarch; stir in shredded orange peel and orange juice. Cook, stirring constantly, over medium heat till thickened and bubbly. Reduce heat; cook and stir 1 minute longer.

    Remove from heat; cool. Blend in yogurt and whipped dessert topping; chill. To serve, spoon over fresh fruit. Makes 1⅔ cups topping. (11 calories/tablespoon.)

Slenderizing Luncheon
Serves 6

Tomato Cocktail
Slim Ham Slaw
Carrot Curls   Green Onions
Oatmeal Breadsticks
Fresh Fruit   Yogurt Topping
Iced Tea

BUFFET SERVING TIP: To make the table look bountiful while keeping in mind the goals of dieting guests, select a buffet table just large enough for serving. By doing this, the food on the table won't look skimpy.

Slim Ham Slaw

   2 tablespoons all-purpose flour
   2 tablespoons sugar
   1 teaspoon salt
   1 teaspoon dry mustard
   ½ teaspoon celery seed
   1 cup skim milk
   2 slightly beaten egg yolks
   3 tablespoons vinegar
   2 tablespoons lemon juice
   1 large head cabbage
   2 cups cubed fully cooked ham
   1 apple, cored and cut in thin wedges
   ¼ cup chopped green pepper
   ¼ cup sliced radish

In saucepan mix flour, sugar, salt, mustard, and celery seed; slowly stir in milk. Cook and stir till thick and bubbly. Stir a moderate amount of hot mixture into yolks; return to saucepan. Cook and stir over low heat 1 minute. Stir in vinegar and lemon juice; cool. Spread apart outer leaves of cabbage. Carefully cut out center, leaving a ½-inch-thick shell to form 'bowl'. Shred removed cabbage to make 4 cups; toss with ham, apple, green pepper, and radish. Toss with cooked mixture; serve in cabbage shell. Makes 6 servings. (178 calories/serving.)

Oatmeal Breadsticks

   3 cups all-purpose flour
   1 package active dry yeast
1¼ cups water
   2 tablespoons shortening
   1 tablespoon sugar
   1 cup quick-cooking rolled oats
   2 tablespoons butter, melted

In large mixing bowl stir together *1½ cups* of the flour and the yeast. Heat together water, shortening, sugar, and 1½ teaspoons salt just till warm (115° to 120°); stir to melt shortening. Add to flour mixture. Beat at low speed of electric mixer for ½ minute, scraping bowl constantly. Beat 3 minutes at high speed. By hand stir in remaining flour and oats. Cover; let rise till double (1 to 1½ hours). Punch down; let rest 10 minutes. Shape into 24 sticks, ½ inch thick. Place on greased baking sheet. Let rise till double (about 30 minutes). Bake at 375° for 20 to 25 minutes. Brush with melted butter. Makes 24. (85 calories/breadstick.)

To hollow out cabbage, carefully cut out and remove center of cabbage till a ½-inch-thick shell remains. Serve salad in cabbage 'bowl'.

Salad Bar Luncheon
Serves 12 or more

Herbed Cocktail
Shrimp-Macaroni Salad
Tuna-Rice Salad
Turkey-Mushroom Salad
Marinated Vegetable Combo
Cinnamon Fruit Salad
Peach-Pineapple Ring
Nut Bread   Butter
Mandarin Meringues
Coffee

BUFFET SERVING TIP: Organize a salad buffet for your next club luncheon. Let committee members bring the salads and breads; you can prepare the appetizer and dessert. To make it a fund-raising affair, add more salads to the buffet and invite paying guests.

Turkey-Mushroom Salad

In large bowl combine 5 cups cubed cooked turkey, 3 cups sliced fresh mushrooms, 2 cups chopped celery, and ¼ cup sliced pimiento-stuffed olives. Blend together ⅔ cup mayonnaise or salad dressing, 2 tablespoons lemon juice, 2 teaspoons finely chopped onion, and 1 teaspoon salt. Add to turkey mixture; toss lightly. Chill thoroughly. Line salad bowl with romaine leaves; spoon in chilled turkey salad. Makes 12 servings.

Nut Bread

In mixing bowl thoroughly stir together 3 cups all-purpose flour, 1 cup sugar, 4 teaspoons baking powder, and 1 teaspoon salt. Combine 1 beaten egg, 1½ cups milk, and ¼ cup cooking oil. Add to dry ingredients, beating well. Stir in ¾ cup chopped walnuts. Turn batter into greased 8½x4½x2½-inch loaf pan. Bake at 350° about 70 minutes. Remove from pan; cool on rack. Makes 1 loaf.

Herbed Cocktail

In saucepan combine one 24-ounce can vegetable juice cocktail; two 13¾-ounce cans chicken broth; 2 to 4 drops bottled hot pepper sauce; and ½ teaspoon dried basil, crushed. Bring to a boil; simmer 10 minutes. Serve hot. If desired, top each serving with a pat of butter or margarine. Serves 12.

Tuna-Rice Salad

    2 10-ounce packages frozen peas
 1½ cups long grain rice
    2 9¼-ounce cans tuna, drained
    2 8½-ounce cans pineapple tidbits,
        drained
    1 cup chopped celery
    1 cup Thousand Island dressing
    1 cup dairy sour cream
  ¼ cup finely chopped green onion

Cook peas and rice according to package directions; drain. In large bowl combine peas, rice, tuna, pineapple, and celery. Mix remaining ingredients; pour over rice mixture. Toss lightly. Cover; chill 12 to 24 hours. Toss again. If desired, serve in lettuce-lined salad bowl. Makes 12 servings.

Shrimp-Macaroni Salad

    2 pounds shelled shrimp, cooked
 1½ cups macaroni shells, cooked and
        drained (3 cups)
    2 cups cubed American cheese (8 ounces)
    1 cup chopped celery
  ½ cup chopped green pepper
  ¼ cup chopped onion
    1 cup mayonnaise or salad dressing
    1 cup dairy sour cream
    6 tablespoons vinegar
 1½ teaspoons salt
        Dash bottled hot pepper sauce

Cut up shrimp; toss with cooked macaroni, cheese, and vegetables. Blend remaining ingredients; toss with shrimp mixture. Cover; chill thoroughly. Stir. If desired, top with green pepper rings. Makes 12 servings.

Cinnamon Fruit Salad

¼ cup red cinnamon candies
2 tablespoons vinegar
3 beaten egg yolks
2 tablespoons honey
1 tablespoon butter or margarine
1 tablespoon lemon juice
2 cups sliced banana
3 cups diced unpeeled apple
1 cup tiny marshmallows
1 cup halved seedless green grapes
½ cup whipping cream

In small saucepan combine candies, vinegar, 2 tablespoons water, and dash salt; cook and stir till candies are dissolved. Combine yolks and honey. Gradually stir hot mixture into yolks; return to saucepan. Add butter. Cook and stir till thickened, 3 to 4 minutes; cool. In large bowl sprinkle lemon juice over banana; let stand a few minutes. Add apple, marshmallows, and grapes. Whip cream; fold into yolk mixture. Fold whipped cream mixture into fruit. Chill several hours or overnight. Makes 10 to 12 servings.

Peach-Pineapple Ring

3 3-ounce packages lemon-flavored gelatin
2 cups boiling water
1 29-ounce can peach halves
1 29½-ounce can pineapple slices
½ cup drained maraschino cherries (20)

Dissolve gelatin in boiling water. Drain peaches and pineapple, reserving syrups. Combine syrups; add enough cold water to make 3 cups. Add syrup mixture to dissolved gelatin. Chill till partially set.

Alternate peaches, cut side up, and some of the cherries in bottom of a 12-cup ring mold. Gently pour *2 cups* partially set gelatin over; chill till *almost* firm. Keep remaining gelatin at room temperature. Halve pineapple slices; place, cut edge down, around outside and inside of mold to make "scalloped" design. Center remaining cherries in pineapple half rings. Gently pour remaining gelatin over. Chill till firm. Makes 12 to 16 servings.

Marinated Vegetable Combo

1 16-ounce can whole kernel corn, drained
1 8½-ounce can peas, drained
1 8½-ounce can lima beans, drained
1 8-ounce can cut green beans, drained
½ cup finely diced green pepper
¼ cup chopped canned pimiento
¾ cup vinegar
½ cup sugar
½ cup salad oil
1 teaspoon salt
½ teaspoon dried dillweed
⅛ teaspoon pepper
Hard-cooked egg wedges

Combine corn, peas, lima beans, green beans, green pepper, and pimiento. Blend vinegar, sugar, oil, salt, dillweed, and pepper. Pour over vegetables. Chill; stir occasionally. Garnish with egg wedges. Serves 10 to 12.

Mandarin Meringues

4 egg whites
¼ teaspoon cream of tartar
1 cup sugar
1 teaspoon vanilla
Mandarin Filling

Have egg whites at room temperature; beat with cream of tartar to soft peaks. Add sugar, a little at a time, beating till very stiff peaks form and sugar is dissolved. Cover 2 baking sheets with brown paper. On each paper draw 6 circles, each about 3 inches in diameter. Spread each circle with a little meringue, shaping into a shell with back of spoon. Bake at 275° for 1 hour. Turn off heat; let shells dry in oven with door closed 1 to 2 hours. Fill with Mandarin Filling. Makes 12 servings.

Mandarin Filling: Drain six 11-ounce *or* four 16-ounce cans mandarin orange sections, reserving 1½ cups syrup. In medium saucepan combine 3 tablespoons sugar and 5 teaspoons cornstarch; slowly stir in reserved syrup. Cook and stir till thickened and bubbly. Stir in oranges, 3 tablespoons lemon juice, and ½ teaspoon ground ginger. Cool slightly.

Bridge Luncheon
Serves 8

Polynesian Platter
Lime-Sesame Dressing
Orange-Pineapple Dressing
Whole Wheat Muffins
or
Granola Muffins
Butter   Jelly
Toasted Coconut Mold
Minted Iced Tea

BUFFET SERVING TIP: To dramatize colorful buffet foods use clear glass plates and serving dishes. Let guests dine at cloth-covered card tables, then clear tables and remove cloths for an afternoon of bridge.

Toasted Coconut Mold

⅓ cup sugar
1 envelope unflavored gelatin
¼ teaspoon salt
1½ cups milk
2 beaten egg yolks
½ teaspoon vanilla
¼ teaspoon almond extract
1 5⅓-ounce can evaporated milk (⅔ cup)
2 stiffly beaten egg whites
½ cup flaked coconut, toasted

In small saucepan combine sugar, unflavored gelatin, and salt; stir in milk and beaten egg yolks. Cook and stir over low heat till mixture thickens slightly and coats a metal spoon. Add vanilla and almond extract. Chill mixture till partially set.

Meanwhile, pour evaporated milk into freezer tray. Freeze till edges of milk are icy; whip to stiff peaks. Gently fold beaten egg whites, *half* of the toasted coconut, and whipped milk into gelatin mixture. Turn into a 6-cup mold; chill till firm.

To serve, unmold onto serving plate; sprinkle with remaining coconut. Serves 8.

Polynesian Platter

1 slightly beaten egg white
1 tablespoon water
1 small bunch seedless green grapes, divided into clusters
¼ cup sugar
1 honeydew melon, peeled and sliced
1 papaya *or* cantaloupe, peeled and sliced
1 pineapple, peeled, eyes removed, cored, and cut in chunks
1 pint whole strawberries
16 slices boiled ham
Watercress

Combine egg white and water; brush over grapes. Sprinkle with sugar; dry on rack.

Arrange assorted fruits at each end of large platter. Roll up ham; arrange in center of platter. Garnish with watercress. Chill. Serve with Lime-Sesame Dressing and Orange-Pineapple Dressing. Serves 8.

Lime-Sesame Dressing

½ cup salad oil
½ teaspoon grated lime peel
3 tablespoons lime juice
1 tablespoon sesame seed, toasted
½ teaspoon dry mustard
¼ teaspoon salt
1 drop green food coloring

In screw-top jar combine oil, peel, juice, sesame seed, mustard, salt, and food coloring; shake well. Chill. Makes ¾ cup.

Orange-Pineapple Dressing

¼ teaspoon grated orange peel
¼ cup orange juice
2 teaspoons sugar
Dash ground cinnamon
1 8-ounce carton pineapple yogurt

Combine grated peel, orange juice, sugar, and cinnamon; stir into pineapple yogurt. Garnish with additional orange peel, if desired. Makes about 1 cup dressing.

Polynesian Platter is as pretty as it is refreshing on a hot day. Guests have a choice of tangy *Lime-Sesame Dressing* or spicy *Orange-Pineapple Dressing*—don't be surprised if they want to sample both.

Whole Wheat Muffins

  1½ cups whole wheat flour
  ½ cup all-purpose flour
  ¼ cup shelled pumpkin seeds, chopped
2½ teaspoons baking powder
  ¾ teaspoon salt
  1 beaten egg
  ¾ cup milk
  ⅓ cup cooking oil
  ⅓ cup light molasses

In mixing bowl thoroughly stir together flours, pumpkin seeds, baking powder, and salt. Combine beaten egg, milk, oil, and molasses. Make a well in dry ingredients; stir in egg mixture just till dry ingredients are moistened. Fill greased muffin pans ⅔ full with batter. Bake muffins at 400° till done, 20 to 25 minutes. Makes 12 muffins.

Granola Muffins

1¾ cups all-purpose flour
  ½ cup whole wheat flour
  1 cup granola with raisins
  ½ cup packed brown sugar
  3 teaspoons baking powder
  ¼ teaspoon salt
  1 slightly beaten egg
  1 cup milk
  ¼ cup cooking oil

In mixing bowl thoroughly stir together all-purpose flour, whole wheat flour, granola, sugar, baking powder, and salt. Combine egg, milk, and oil. Make a well in dry ingredients; stir in egg mixture just till dry ingredients are moistened. Fill greased muffin pans ⅔ full with batter. Bake at 400° for 20 to 25 minutes. Makes 12 muffins.

Ladies' Buffet

Serves 6

Salmon-Cheese Bake
Asparagus with Cashews
Lemon Yogurt Mold
Raisin-Coconut Bars
Coffee

BUFFET SERVING TIP: To make baked dishes easier to serve, cut into serving-size pieces before placing on buffet. Or, transfer serving pieces from pan to warm platter; place platter on warming tray on table.

Raisin-Coconut Bars

¾ cup butter or margarine, softened
½ cup granulated sugar
½ teaspoon salt
2 cups all purpose flour

• • •

3 eggs
1 teaspoon vanilla
1 cup packed brown sugar
3 tablespoons all-purpose flour
½ teaspoon salt
1 cup raisins
½ cup shredded coconut
1 cup sifted powdered sugar
½ teaspoon vanilla
Milk

Cream together butter, granulated sugar, and ½ teaspoon salt. Stir in 2 cups flour. Pat onto bottom of 13x9x2-inch baking pan. Bake at 350° till lightly browned, about 20 minutes. Beat eggs slightly; add 1 teaspoon vanilla. Gradually add brown sugar, beating just till blended. Add 3 tablespoons flour and ½ teaspoon salt. Stir in raisins and coconut. Spread over baked layer. Bake at 350° till golden brown, 20 to 25 minutes. Combine powdered sugar, ½ teaspoon vanilla, and enough milk to make of glaze consistency. Drizzle over warm cookies. Cool; cut into bars. Makes 36.

Salmon-Cheese Bake

1 16-ounce can salmon, drained and flaked
½ cup finely chopped onion
2 cups packaged biscuit mix
2 slices mozzarella cheese
2 tablespoons grated Parmesan cheese
1 10½-ounce can condensed cream of celery soup
¼ cup milk
¼ teaspoon dried dillweed

Combine salmon and onion; set aside. Combine biscuit mix and ½ cup water; divide in half. Roll *half* of dough to an 8-inch square. Fit into bottom of greased 8x8x2-inch baking pan. Top with salmon mixture, then mozzarella. Roll remaining dough to 8-inch square; place over cheese. Sprinkle with Parmesan. Bake at 450° for 15 to 18 minutes. Heat together soup, milk, and dillweed. To serve, cut casserole in squares. Serve with warm sauce. Makes 6 servings.

Asparagus with Cashews

Cook two 9-ounce packages frozen asparagus spears according to package directions; drain. In small skillet cook ¼ cup coarsely chopped cashew nuts in 2 tablespoons butter over low heat till butter is lightly browned. Spoon over asparagus. Serves 6.

Lemon Yogurt Mold

1 3-ounce package lemon-flavored gelatin
1 8¼-ounce can crushed pineapple
1 8-ounce carton lemon yogurt
1 large cucumber, peeled, seeded, and shredded (1 cup)

Dissolve gelatin in 1 cup boiling water. Drain pineapple; reserve syrup. Add cold water to reserved syrup to make ⅔ cup. Stir syrup into gelatin; cool. With rotary beater, beat yogurt into gelatin; chill till partially set. Fold in fruit and cucumber. Pour into 4-cup mold; chill till firm. Makes 6 servings.

Bargain Buffet
Serves 8 (halve for 4)

Apple-Tuna Casserole
Belgian Tossed Salad
Tomato Wedges   Cucumber Slices
Assorted Rolls   Butter
Nutty Chocolate Cookies
Hot Tea

BUFFET SERVING TIP: To keep entertaining costs low, make imaginative place mats or table runners from colorful discarded sheets or curtains. For an instant centerpiece, move a terrarium, herb garden, potted plant, or figurine to the buffet table.

Apple-Tuna Casserole

    1 7-ounce package macaroni
        (2 cups)
    6 tablespoons butter or margarine
    ¼ cup all-purpose flour
    ¾ teaspoon salt
    3 cups milk
    2 cups shredded sharp American
        cheese (8 ounces)
    2 6½- or 7-ounce cans tuna, drained
    3 or 4 tart apples, cored,
        peeled, and diced
    ½ cup soft bread crumbs
    2 tablespoons butter or margarine,
        melted

Cook macaroni according to package directions; drain. In saucepan melt 6 tablespoons butter over low heat. Blend in flour and salt. Add milk all at once. Cook and stir till thick and bubbly. Stir in cheese till melted. Stir in tuna, apple, and macaroni; turn into a 12x7½ x2-inch baking dish.

Combine crumbs and melted butter. Sprinkle atop casserole. Bake at 350° till apples are tender, 30 minutes. Serves 8.
To serve 4: Use half recipe, *except* use 2 diced apples. Bake in 1-quart casserole.

Belgian Tossed Salad

    1 10-ounce package frozen Brussels
        sprouts
    ½ cup salad oil
    ¼ cup vinegar
    1 clove garlic, crushed
    1 teaspoon dried parlsey flakes,
        crushed
    ½ teaspoon salt
    ¼ teaspoon dried basil, crushed
    ⅛ teaspoon pepper
    8 cups torn mixed salad greens
    ½ medium red onion, sliced and
        separated into rings
    6 slices bacon, crisp-cooked, drained,
        and crumbled

Cook Brussels sprouts in boiling salted water till barely tender, about 5 minutes; drain. Meanwhile, in screw-top jar combine oil and next 6 ingredients; cover and shake well. Cut Brussels sprouts in half lengthwise; pour marinade over. Chill.

In salad bowl arrange greens, onion rings, and bacon. Add Brussels sprouts with marinade; toss gently. Makes 8 servings.

Nutty Chocolate Cookies

    1½ cups semisweet chocolate pieces
    ¾ cup sugar
    ¼ cup butter or margarine
    1 egg
    1½ teaspoons vanilla
    ½ cup all-purpose flour
    ½ teaspoon salt
    ¼ teaspoon baking powder
    ½ cup chopped walnuts

In small saucepan melt *1 cup* of the chocolate over low heat; cool. In small mixing bowl cream together sugar and butter; add egg and vanilla. Beat well. Blend in melted chocolate. Thoroughly stir together flour, salt, and baking powder. Add to creamed mixture; mix well. Stir in nuts and remaining chocolate pieces. Drop dough from a teaspoon, two inches apart, onto lightly greased cookie sheet. Bake at 350° for 8 to 10 minutes. Makes 30 cookies.

Little League Lunch
Serves 8

Tomato-Lima Soup
Corn-Stuffed Franks
Crisp Carrot and Celery Sticks
Blueberry-Ginger Cakes
Milk

BUFFET SERVING TIP: Serve the buffet on the patio or in area away from family activities so that the boys can talk about the game without interruption. Use ball game mementos to set the mood, such as marking cushions as bases for seating and inserting miniature pennants in franks or cupcakes.

Corn-Stuffed Franks

Slice 1 pound frankfurters (8 to 10) lengthwise almost to opposite side. In medium bowl combine 1½ cups herb-seasoned stuffing mix, one 8¾-ounce can cream-style corn, ½ cup shredded American cheese (2 ounces), ⅓ cup water, and 2 teaspoons prepared mustard. Mix thoroughly.

Mound about ¼ cup stuffing mixture atop each slit frankfurter. Place stuffing-topped franks on baking sheet. Bake at 400° for 10 minutes. Makes 8 to 10 servings.

To stuff frankfurters, slit lengthwise almost to opposite side. Force frank halves to lay flat, then spoon stuffing mixture on top.

Tomato-Lima Soup

1½ cups dry baby lima beans
1 16-ounce can tomatoes, cut up
1 8-ounce can tomato sauce
1 cup finely chopped onion
1 cup finely chopped celery
2 vegetable bouillon cubes
1 teaspoon salt
½ teaspoon chili powder
¼ teaspoon Worcestershire sauce

Rinse beans; place in large saucepan with 6 cups water. Bring to a boil; simmer for 2 minutes. Remove from heat; let stand 1 hour. Do not drain. Add remaining ingredients; bring to a boil. Reduce heat; simmer, covered, till beans are tender, 1½ to 2 hours. Mash beans slightly with potato masher. Serves 8.

Blueberry-Ginger Cakes

1 cup fresh or frozen blueberries
¾ cup sugar
½ cup butter or margarine
1 egg
¼ cup molasses
2 cups all-purpose flour
1 teaspoon baking powder
1 teaspoon ground cinnamon
½ teaspoon baking soda
½ teaspoon salt
½ teaspoon ground ginger
1 cup buttermilk
Lemon Butter Frosting

Thaw and drain berries, if frozen. Cream together sugar and butter. Add egg; beat well. Stir in molasses. Stir together flour and next 5 ingredients. Add alternately to creamed mixture with buttermilk; mix well. Fold in berries. Fill paper bake cups in muffin pans ⅔ full. Bake at 350° for 20 to 25 minutes. Cool. Frost cooled cupcakes with Lemon Butter Frosting. Makes 18.

Lemon Butter Frosting: Cream ¼ cup butter. Gradually add 2 cups sifted powdered sugar; blend smooth. Add 1 teaspoon grated lemon peel and 1 tablespoon lemon juice; beat smooth. Stir in enough milk (1 to 2 teaspoons) to make of spreading consistency.

Chowder Break

Serves 6

Cheesy Bean Chowder
Spicy Pickled Onion Rings
Tossed Salad
Herb Loaf   Butter
Brownie-Nut Torte
Milk

BUFFET SERVING TIP: Keep chowder warm on the buffet table in an electric soup tureen, fondue pot, or Dutch oven placed on a warming tray. To eliminate the need for knives, slice bread loaf and butter; wrap in foil and heat in the oven for a few minutes. Serve bread hot from foil packet.

Cheesy Bean Chowder

2½ cups dry pinto beans (16 ounces)
2 beef bouillon cubes
½ teaspoon dried thyme, crushed
¼ teaspoon salt
   Dash pepper
2 cups diced carrots
4 cups milk
¼ cup all-purpose flour
1 cup shredded sharp American
   cheese (4 ounces)
4 slices bacon, crisp-cooked, drained,
   and crumbled

Rinse beans; place in large saucepan with 6 cups water. Bring to a boil; simmer for 2 minutes. Remove from heat; let stand in water 1 hour. Do not drain. Add bouillon cubes, thyme, salt, and pepper. Bring to a boil. Reduce heat; cover and simmer 1 hour. Add carrots; cover and simmer ½ hour. Mash beans slightly with potato masher.

Blend about *1 cup* milk into flour; add to beans with remaining milk. Cook and stir till thick and bubbly. Add cheese; heat and stir till melted. Season to taste. Serve garnished with crumbled bacon. Makes 6 servings.

Spicy Pickled Onion Rings

Serve beets later as a vegetable or in a salad—

1 16-ounce can beets
1½ cups white vinegar
¼ cup sugar
6 inches stick cinnamon, broken up
2 teaspoons whole cloves
1 pound large red onions, sliced and
   separated into rings (about 4 cups)

Drain beets, reserving juice. Add water to beet juice to make 1½ cups. Add vinegar, sugar, cinnamon, cloves, and ½ teaspoon salt. Simmer, covered, for 10 minutes. Strain; pour hot mixture over onions. Cover and chill 6 hours or overnight; stir occasionally. Drain before serving. Makes 4 cups.

Herb Loaf

Thaw one 16-ounce loaf frozen bread dough for 1½ to 2 hours. Roll to 12x9-inch rectangle. Combine ¼ cup butter or margarine, softened; 2 tablespoons spaghetti sauce mix; and 2 tablespoons snipped parsley. Spread on dough. Roll jelly-roll fashion, beginning with long side; seal. Place, seam side down, on greased baking sheet. Brush with water; sprinkle with a little salt.

Let rise till almost double (about 1 hour). Make shallow slashes across top at 2-inch intervals. Bake at 375° till done, about 30 minutes. Makes 1 loaf.

Brownie-Nut Torte

1 16-ounce package brownie mix
¾ cup chopped nuts
2 cups frozen whipped dessert topping

Prepare mix according to package directions, *except* stir in ½ cup nuts. Spread in 2 greased and floured 8x1½-inch round baking pans. Bake at 350° for 20 minutes. Remove from pans; cool thoroughly. Thaw topping; spread *1 cup* atop one brownie layer. Top with second layer; spread remaining topping on second layer. Sprinkle with remaining nuts. Chill 1 hour. Serves 6 to 8.

Evening Dinners

Oriental Buffet
Serves 8

Appetizer Egg Rolls
Chicken Mandarin   Rice
Oriental Vegetable Tray
Lemon Sherbet   Fortune Cookies
Green Tea   Sake

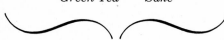

BUFFET SERVING TIP: Add a splash of showmanship to your dinner party by cooking the Chicken Mandarin at the table in an electric skillet or wok. Assemble and cover ingredients on a tray and refrigerate them until it's time for the main course. Whisk utensils out to the kitchen while the finished dish heats through.

Oriental Vegetable Tray

½ cup water
2 tablespoons sugar
2 tablespoons soy sauce
1 tablespoon vinegar
2 6-ounce packages frozen pea pods, cooked and drained
1 8-ounce can water chestnuts, drained and sliced
6 ounces fresh mushrooms, halved
Lettuce
1 large cucumber, scored and thinly sliced (1½ cups)
4 tomatoes, cut in wedges

Mix water, sugar, soy sauce, and vinegar. Pour over pea pods and chestnuts in shallow dish. Cover. Chill; stir occasionally. To serve, mound mushrooms in center of large lettuce-lined tray. Drain peas and chestnuts; arrange with cucumber and tomatoes on tray. Pass soy sauce, if desired. Serves 8.

Chicken Mandarin

4 whole chicken breasts, skinned, boned, and halved lengthwise
1 large green pepper
6 green onions
2 tablespoons cooking oil
1 13¾-ounce can chicken broth

• • •

1 11-ounce can mandarin orange sections
¼ cup packed brown sugar
¼ cup soy sauce
3 tablespoons vinegar
⅓ cup cornstarch
1 teaspoon grated gingerroot *or* ¼ teaspoon ground ginger
Hot cooked rice
Soy sauce (optional)

Cut chicken breasts and green pepper into ½-inch-wide strips; bias-slice green onions. In wok, electric skillet, or large skillet quickly cook and stir chicken strips over medium-high heat in hot oil till browned. Add green pepper strips, sliced onion, and chicken broth; bring mixture to a boil. Reduce heat; cover. Cook 2 to 3 minutes.

Meanwhile, drain mandarin oranges, reserving syrup. Combine reserved orange syrup, brown sugar, soy sauce, and vinegar; slowly blend into cornstarch and grated gingerroot or ground ginger. Add brown sugar mixture to chicken mixture; cook, stirring constantly, till mixture is thickened and bubbly. Stir in mandarin orange sections; cover and heat through. Serve chicken mixture over hot cooked rice. Pass additional soy sauce, if desired. Makes 8 servings.

Foods with faraway flair

Although the *Chicken Mandarin* and the *Oriental Vegetable Tray* have Far Eastern origins, the ingredients come from the neighborhood supermarket where you also buy the fortune cookies.

Saturday Night Dinner
Serves 12 (halve for 6)

Oven-Easy Barbecued Chicken
Ham   Orange-Chestnut Rice
Hot Vegetable Platter
Tossed Green Salad
Hard Rolls   Butter
Angel Cake
Coffee

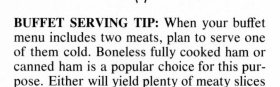

BUFFET SERVING TIP: When your buffet menu includes two meats, plan to serve one of them cold. Boneless fully cooked ham or canned ham is a popular choice for this purpose. Either will yield plenty of meaty slices without requiring special carving skills.

Hot Vegetable Platter

    1 head cauliflower
    1 pound carrots, cut in thin strips
    2 tablespoons butter or margarine
    2 9-ounce packages frozen Italian
        green beans
    4 tomatoes, cut in thick slices
        Easy Cheese Sauce
    1 slice bacon, crisp-cooked, drained,
        and crumbled

Cook whole cauliflower, covered, in a small amount of boiling salted water for 20 minutes; drain. Cook carrots, covered, in small amount of boiling salted water for 20 minutes; drain. Stir in *1 tablespoon* of the butter. Cook beans following package directions; drain. Stir in remaining butter. Season tomatoes; heat in baking dish at 350° for 5 minutes. Arrange hot vegetables on large platter. Spoon some Easy Cheese Sauce over cauliflower; sprinkle bacon atop. Serve remaining sauce with cauliflower. Serves 12.
    Easy Cheese Sauce: In saucepan combine one 11-ounce can condensed Cheddar cheese soup, 1 cup dairy sour cream, and 1 teaspoon prepared mustard. Heat till bubbly.

Oven-Easy Barbecued Chicken
Featured in the buffet menu on the cover—

    3 2½- to 3-pound ready-to-cook
        broiler-fryer chickens, cut up
    ½ cup butter or margarine, melted
    1 cup bottled barbecue sauce

Line two large, shallow baking pans with foil. Place chicken pieces in a single layer, skin side up, in pans. Brush chicken lightly with *half* of the melted butter. Bake, uncovered, at 375° for 50 minutes. Combine remaining butter with barbecue sauce; brush on chicken. Bake, uncovered, till done, about 10 minutes more. If it is necessary to keep chicken warm up to 1 hour, cover with foil; reduce oven heat to 200°. Serves 12.

Orange-Chestnut Rice
Water chestnuts give a delightful crunchiness—

    3¾ cups water
    ½ of a 6-ounce can frozen orange juice
        concentrate (⅓ cup)
    2 teaspoons salt
    1 14-ounce package precooked rice
    1 5-ounce can water chestnuts, drained,
        thinly sliced, and quartered

In large saucepan bring water, orange juice concentrate, butter, and salt to boiling. Add rice and water chestnuts. Return mixture to boiling, stirring occasionally. Remove pan from heat. Let stand, covered, 10 minutes. Transfer to serving bowl. Serves 12.

Tossed Green Salad

In screw-top jar combine ⅔ cup salad oil, ⅓ cup vinegar, 1 tablespoon sugar, ½ teaspoon salt, ⅛ teaspoon garlic powder, and dash pepper; cover and shake well. In large salad bowl toss together 1 large head lettuce, torn in bite-size pieces (about 8 cups); 8 ounces fresh spinach, torn in bite-size pieces; ¼ cup sliced green onion; and 3 hard-cooked eggs, coarsely chopped. Before serving, toss salad with desired amount of dressing. Serves 12.

Buffet for a Crowd

Serves 24 (halve for 12)

Buffet Chicken Scallop
Roast Pork
Candied Sweet Potatoes
Vegetable Wreath Salad
Sliced Tomatoes
Corn Relish   Ripe Olives
Buttered French Bread
Summer Fruit Bowl
Iced Tea   Coffee

BUFFET SERVING TIP: Give the host a chance to show his expertise with a carving knife. Let him slice the pork roast at the table. To avoid overcrowding the buffet, serve the beverage from a tea cart or small table.

Vegetable Wreath Salad

4 16-ounce cans whole green beans
1 large red onion
2 cups sliced fresh mushrooms
½ cup salad oil
2 tablespoons vinegar
2 tablespoons lemon juice
2 teaspoons sugar
½ teaspoon salt
½ teaspoon paprika
½ teaspoon dry mustard
Dash cayenne
Bibb or other lettuce
1 16-ounce can sweet pickled tiny whole beets, chilled and drained

Drain beans. Chop *half* of the onion; slice remaining and separate into rings. Combine chopped onion, beans, and mushrooms. In screw-top jar combine oil and next 7 ingredients. Cover and shake well. Add to bean mixture; toss gently. Chill thoroughly.

Arrange lettuce on large, round platter or in large, shallow salad bowl. Mound bean mixture in center; top with onion rings. Surround with beets. Serves 24.

Buffet Chicken Scallop

2 medium onions, chopped (1 cup)
1 large green pepper, chopped (1 cup)
2 tablespoons butter or margarine
1 16-ounce package herb-seasoned stuffing mix
4 cups chicken broth
6 beaten eggs
3 10½-ounce cans condensed cream of celery soup
8 cups diced cooked chicken (2 pounds)
1 cup long grain rice, cooked (3 cups)
1 4-ounce can diced pimiento, drained
2 10½-ounce cans condensed cream of chicken soup
½ cup milk
1 cup dairy sour cream

Cook onions and green pepper in butter till tender but not brown. In large mixing bowl toss together stuffing mix, broth, eggs, and celery soup; add chicken, rice, onions, green pepper, and pimiento. Mix well. Turn into 2 greased 13x9x2-inch baking dishes. Bake at 325° for 30 to 40 minutes.

In saucepan combine chicken soup and milk, heat and stir till smooth. Stir in sour cream; heat through *but do not boil.* To serve, cut casserole into squares; spoon sauce over each serving. Serves 24.

Summer Fruit Bowl

3 cups cantaloupe balls
3 cups honeydew melon balls
1 pineapple, peeled, eyes removed, cored, and diced (3 cups)
1 quart strawberries, halved (4 cups)
1 pint blueberries (2 cups)
2 kiwi, peeled and diced (1 cup)
1 cup apricot preserves
⅔ cup hot water
½ cup orange liqueur
½ of a 6-ounce can frozen orange juice concentrate (⅓ cup)

Chill fruits; layer in compote or large glass bowl. Combine apricot preserves, hot water, liqueur, and concentrate; drizzle over fruit. Chill thoroughly. Serves 24.

Smorgasbord

Serves 18

Pickled Herring
Sardine Appetizer Spread
Deviled Eggs   Cheese Tray
Jellied Veal (Kalvsylta)
Cucumbers in Sour Cream
Swedish Meatballs
Potato Sausage
Creamed Potatoes with Dill
Swedish Brown Beans
Cranberry or Lingonberry Sauce
Toasted Almond Sponge
Assorted Cookies
Coffee

BUFFET SERVING TIP: To serve a smorgasbord in the traditional style, you should provide clean plates for each of the food groups —fish and appetizers; cold meats and salads; hot meats and vegetables; and desserts.

Toasted Almond Sponge

2 envelopes unflavored gelatin
2 cups sugar
2½ cups milk, scalded
1 teaspoon salt
2 teaspoons vanilla
2 cups whipping cream
1 cup toasted slivered almonds

Soften gelatin in 1 cup cold water. In heavy skillet caramelize *1½ cups* of the sugar, stirring constantly so it doesn't burn. Remove from heat when deep golden brown. Slowly add milk. Cook and stir till all caramel dissolves. Remove from heat.

Add softened gelatin, remaining sugar, and salt; stir till dissolved. Stir in vanilla. Pour into bowl; chill till thick and syrupy. Whip cream; fold into gelatin. Fold in nuts. Turn into two 4½-cup molds. Chill till firm, overnight. Unmold onto serving platters. Makes 18 to 20 servings.

Jellied Veal (Kalvsylta)

1 2- to 3-pound bone-in veal shoulder
2 veal or pigs knuckles (2½ pounds)
1 large onion, sliced
1 large carrot, sliced
2 sprigs parsley
1 tablespoon salt
10 whole allspice
10 whole peppercorns
2 bay leaves
1 tablespoon white vinegar
¼ teaspoon white pepper

Have meat bones in shoulder and knuckles cracked in several places by meatman. In large kettle or Dutch oven place meats and 3 quarts cold water; bring to boiling. Add onion, carrot, parsley, salt, allspice, peppercorns, and bay leaves. Cover; simmer till meat is very tender, 2 to 2½ hours.

Remove meat from stock; cut meat from bones. Return bones to stock and boil, uncovered, till stock is reduced to 6 cups, 45 minutes to 1 hour. Meanwhile, cut meat into very small pieces, trimming away any gristle. Strain stock; add meat (about 4 cups), vinegar, and white pepper. Chill till partially set; remove all fat from surface. Pour mixture into two 7½x3½x2-inch loaf pans. Chill 5 to 6 hours or overnight. Unmold and slice for serving. Makes 2 loaves.

Creamed Potatoes with Dill

6 pounds tiny new potatoes, peeled
¼ cup butter or margarine
3 tablespoons all-purpose flour
1 teaspoon dried dillweed
3 cups light cream
1⅓ cups milk

In large kettle bring potatoes to a boil in salted water. Cover. Reduce heat; cook till tender, 15 to 20 minutes. Drain well; return to kettle. Keep warm. In saucepan melt butter; blend in flour, dillweed, and 2 teaspoons salt. Add cream and milk all at once. Cook and stir till thick and bubbly. Pour over potatoes; heat through. If desired, sprinkle with additional dillweed. Serves 18 to 20.

Swedish Meatballs

¾ pound lean ground beef
½ pound ground veal
¼ pound ground pork
1½ cups soft bread crumbs
1 cup light cream
½ cup chopped onion
3 tablespoons butter or margarine
1 egg
¼ cup finely snipped parsley
1¼ teaspoons salt
Dash ground ginger
Dash ground nutmeg
Gravy

Have meats ground together twice. Soak the bread crumbs in cream about 5 minutes. In saucepan cook onion in *1 tablespoon* of the butter till tender but not brown.

Mix meats, bread-crumb mixture, onion, egg, parsley, salt, ginger, nutmeg, and dash pepper. Beat 5 minutes at medium speed of electric mixer, or mix by hand till well combined. Shape into 1-inch balls. (Mixture will be soft. For easier shaping, wet hands or chill the mixture first.) In skillet brown the meatballs in remaining butter. Remove from skillet and prepare Gravy. Add meatballs to Gravy. Cover; cook *slowly*, about 30 minutes. Baste meatballs occasionally with Gravy. Makes about 48.

Gravy: In skillet with drippings, melt 2 tablespoons butter or margarine. Stir in 2 tablespoons all-purpose flour. Dissolve 1 beef bouillon cube in 1¼ cups boiling water. Add bouillon and ½ teaspoon instant coffee powder to flour mixture. Cook, stirring constantly, till thickened and bubbly.

Sardine Appetizer Spread

Drain two 3¾-ounce cans sardines in oil; mash with fork. Combine with ½ cup butter or margarine, softened; ¼ cup finely chopped green onion; ¼ cup chili sauce; 2 tablespoons lemon juice; ½ teaspoon dry mustard; and few drops bottled hot pepper sauce. Blend thoroughly. Chill. Let stand at room temperature a few minutes before serving. Serve with crisp rye wafers. Makes 1½ cups.

Potato Sausage

Beef or pork sausage casings
1½ pounds boneless beef with fat trimmed
1 pound boneless pork with fat trimmed
6 potatoes, peeled and cut up (6 cups)
1 medium onion, cut up
1 tablespoon salt
1 teaspoon ground allspice
¼ teaspoon pepper

Rinse casings; let soak in water 2 hours or overnight. With coarse blade of meat grinder, grind together beef and pork (or ask meatman to grind them together). Combine ground meats, potatoes, onion, salt, allspice, and pepper. Attach sausage stuffer attachment to grinder. Push casing onto stuffer, letting some extend beyond end of attachment. Using coarse plate of grinder, grind mixture together, allowing it to fill casings. Fill casings till firm but not overly full. When link is about 18 inches long, tie ends with string. Before cooking sausage, poke filled casings at intervals with wooden pick to allow fat to escape.

In large saucepan or kettle, cover sausage with water. Cover; cook 30 to 40 minutes. Serve warm. (Cover leftover sausage with water; store in refrigerator. Drain; reheat in oven or skillet.) Makes 5 pounds.

Swedish Brown Beans

3 pounds dry Swedish brown beans
9 inches stick cinnamon
4½ teaspoons salt
1 cup packed brown sugar
¾ cup vinegar
6 tablespoons dark corn syrup

Rinse beans; drain. Place beans in large kettle with 4½ quarts cold water. Cover; let stand overnight. (Or, bring water and beans slowly to boiling; simmer 2 minutes. Cover; let stand 1 hour.) Add cinnamon and salt. Cover; simmer till almost tender, 1½ to 2 hours. Add sugar and vinegar. Cook, uncovered, till tender and desired consistency, about 30 minutes; stir occasionally. Remove cinnamon. Stir in dark corn syrup. Serves 18.

Shrimp-Cheese Balls

An easy, make-ahead hors d'oeuvre—

    2 3-ounce packages cream cheese,
       softened
1½ teaspoons prepared mustard
    1 teaspoon grated onion
    1 teaspoon lemon juice
     Dash cayenne
     Dash salt
    1 4½-ounce can shrimp, drained and
       broken into pieces (about ¾ cup)
  ⅔ cup chopped salted mixed nuts

In mixing bowl blend together softened cream cheese, prepared mustard, onion, lemon juice, cayenne, and salt. Stir shrimp into cheese mixture. Chill.

   Before serving, shape chilled shrimp mixture into ½-inch balls. Roll balls in chopped mixed nuts. Makes 42.

Sherried Custard Sauce

Spoon custard over sliced fresh fruits such as nectarines, peaches, or strawberries—

    4 beaten egg yolks
    1 cup light cream
   ¾ cup milk
    2 to 3 tablespoons cream sherry
   ¼ cup sugar
     Dash salt

In heavy, medium-sized saucepan combine beaten egg yolks, light cream, milk, and cream sherry. Stir in sugar and salt. Cook over low heat, stirring constantly, until the mixture thickens slightly and coats a metal spoon. Remove pan from heat. Set saucepan at once in a large bowl of ice water. Cool mixture, stirring custard 1 to 2 minutes. Pour custard into bowl; cover and refrigerate till serving time. Makes about 2 cups custard sauce.

Serve *Beef Fillets Wellington* topped with a noble companion, *Golden Tarragon Sauce.* Your guests will feel like royalty. Frozen patty shells provide the pastry covering that tenderly wraps the meat.

Epicurean Buffet
Serves 8

Shrimp-Cheese Balls
Beef Fillets Wellington
Golden Tarragon Sauce
Mushroom-Avocado Duo
Poppy Seed Rolls   Butter
Sliced Nectarines
Sherried Custard Sauce
Coffee

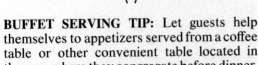

BUFFET SERVING TIP: Let guests help themselves to appetizers served from a coffee table or other convenient table located in the area where they congregate before dinner. Provide small hors d'oeuvre plates and napkins for easier eating. Clear the table as guests move to the buffet for dinner.

Mushroom-Avocado Duo

½ cup salad oil
3 tablespoons tarragon vinegar
2 tablespoons lemon juice
2 tablespoons water
1 tablespoon snipped parsley
1 clove garlic, minced
¾ teaspoon salt
  Dash pepper
• • •
8 ounces fresh mushrooms, halved
  lengthwise (3 cups)
2 avocados, peeled, pitted, and
  sliced
  Parsley sprigs (optional)

In screw-top jar combine salad oil, tarragon vinegar, lemon juice, water, snipped parsley, minced garlic, salt, and pepper. Cover; shake well. Pour over mushrooms and avocados in shallow dish. Refrigerate several hours; spoon marinade over occasionally. At serving time, drain vegetables; arrange on large platter. Garnish with parsley sprigs, if desired. Makes 8 servings.

Beef Fillets Wellington

8 5-ounce fillets of beef
  Cooking oil
1 pound ground beef sirloin
1 clove garlic, crushed
1 tablespoon snipped parsley
8 frozen patty shells, thawed
1 slightly beaten egg white
  Golden Tarragon Sauce

Place fillets in freezer for 20 minutes. Brush with oil; sprinkle with salt and pepper. In hot skillet brown the fillets for 5 minutes on *each* side. Refrigerate.

Combine ground sirloin, garlic, parsley, ½ teaspoon salt, and dash pepper. Divide mixture into 8 portions; place a rounded portion atop *each* fillet. Refrigerate.

Roll *each* patty shell to a 9x5-inch rectangle, ⅛ inch thick. Place one fillet, sirloin side down, on each rectangle. Fold over one side of pastry, then end, then other side, and finally other end; seal. Place, seam side down, in shallow baking pan. Top with cutouts from an additional rolled-out patty shell, if desired. Refrigerate.

Before serving, brush pastry with beaten egg white. Bake at 450° for 10 minutes for rare, 12 minutes for medium-rare, and 15 minutes for medium. Serve with Golden Tarragon Sauce. Makes 8 servings.

Golden Tarragon Sauce

3 egg yolks
½ cup butter or margarine, melted
2 tablespoons lemon juice
2 tablespoons hot water
¼ teaspoon salt
1 teaspoon snipped parsley
⅛ teaspoon dried tarragon, crushed

Beat egg yolks in top of double boiler with wire whisk until smooth but not fluffy. Add butter, lemon juice, hot water, and salt. Place over hot, not boiling, water; beat till sauce begins to thicken, about 5 minutes. Stir in parsley and tarragon. If mixture begins to separate, add a small amount of cold water and beat. Makes about ¾ cup.

New Neighbor Buffet

Serves 8 (double for 16)

Party Dips   Crackers
Meatball Paprikash
Baked Acorn Squash
Fruit-Glazed Carrots
Vinaigrette Greens
Pickled Mushrooms   Celery
Crescent Rolls   Butter
Fresh Strawberries   Cream
Coffee

BUFFET SERVING TIP: Make new neighbors feel welcome by inviting them to a buffet to meet your friends. If group size taxes serving space, you can let the colorful vegetables in the menu double as a centerpiece. Place carrots in a bowl in the center of a large tray and arrange baked squash around it.

Vinaigrette Greens

½ cup salad oil
½ cup white vinegar
¼ cup pimiento-stuffed green olives, cut up
¼ cup snipped parsley
2 tablespoons snipped chives
2 teaspoons sugar
1 teaspoon dry mustard
½ teaspoon salt
⅛ teaspoon cayenne
• • •
6 cups torn greens
16 cherry tomatoes, halved
½ cup coarsely chopped green pepper

In screw-top jar combine salad oil, white vinegar, olives, parsley, chives, sugar, dry mustard, salt, and cayenne. Cover and shake well. Chill thoroughly.

In salad bowl combine torn greens, cherry tomatoes, and chopped green pepper; shake chilled dressing and pour over salad. Toss lightly. Makes 8 servings.

Meatball Paprikash

3 beaten eggs
½ cup milk
2 cups soft bread crumbs (3 slices)
2 teaspoons paprika
1 teaspoon salt
1 teaspoon dry mustard
¼ teaspoon dried thyme, crushed
¼ teaspoon celery seed
⅛ teaspoon pepper
½ pound ground beef
½ pound ground pork
½ pound ground veal
2 6-ounce packages long grain and wild rice mix
1¾ cups cold water
¼ cup all-purpose flour
¾ cup beef broth
1 tablespoon catsup
1 cup dairy sour cream

Combine first 9 ingredients. Add ground meats; mix well. Shape into 40 small balls. Place in shallow baking pan; bake at 350° for 30 minutes. Drain; set aside.

Meanwhile, cook rice mix according to package directions. Slowly blend water into flour. Add beef broth and catsup; cook and stir till thickened and bubbly. Remove from heat. Stir in sour cream. Stir about *half* of the sauce into rice; turn rice mixture into 13x9x2-inch baking dish. Arrange meatballs atop rice; pour remaining sauce over all. Bake, uncovered, at 350° till heated through, 30 to 35 minutes. Makes 8 servings.

To serve 16: Double; bake in two 13x9x2-inch baking dishes for 35 to 40 minutes.

Fruit-Glazed Carrots

Cut 1 pound carrots in half crosswise, then into quarters to form sticks. Combine ½ cup unsweetened pineapple juice, 2 tablespoons lemon juice, 2 tablespoons butter or margarine, ¼ teaspoon salt, and dash pepper. Bring to a boil; add carrots. Reduce heat; cover and simmer 8 minutes. Blend 2 tablespoons cold water into 2 teaspoons cornstarch. Stir into carrots; cook and stir till thick and bubbly. Makes 8 servings.

Make-Ahead Buffet

Serves 8

Buffet Beef Rolls
Potato-Mushroom Bake
Marinated Asparagus Salad
French Rolls   Butter
Fresh Fruit Platter
Red Wine   Coffee

BUFFET SERVING TIP: Prepare these foods (pictured on page 4) well ahead of the party and refrigerate. Bake them while you put the finishing touches on dinner and greet guests.

Buffet Beef Rolls

1 beaten egg
1 teaspoon onion salt
1 teaspoon seasoned salt
  Dash pepper
2 pounds lean ground beef
8 slices Swiss cheese, each 4 inches
    square
8 thin slices Canadian-style bacon
1 egg
1 cup herb-seasoned bread crumbs
  Cooking oil
1 10½-ounce can condensed golden
    mushroom soup
½ cup dry red wine

Combine 1 beaten egg, onion salt, seasoned salt, and pepper. Add meat; mix well. Shape into eight 4-inch-square patties, ¼ inch thick. Press *1* cheese slice atop each, then *1* bacon slice. Roll jelly-roll fashion; seal seam and ends. Beat remaining egg with 2 tablespoons water. Dip rolls into egg, then into crumbs. In skillet brown the rolls in hot oil. Remove to 11x7x1½-inch baking dish; discard oil in skillet. In same skillet heat soup and wine, scraping brown bits. Pour over rolls. Cover; refrigerate. Bake, uncovered, at 350° about 1¼ hours; baste occasionally. (If not chilled, bake 45 minutes.) Serves 8.

Potato-Mushroom Bake

6 to 8 medium potatoes (3 pounds)
1 clove garlic
8 ounces fresh mushrooms, sliced
½ cup butter or margarine
1 cup light cream
2 egg yolks
¼ cup snipped parsley
1 cup soft bread crumbs

Peel potatoes; cook with garlic in boiling salted water. Meanwhile, cook mushrooms in *2 tablespoons* butter till tender. Drain potatoes; discard garlic. Whip potatoes with *4 tablespoons* butter, cream, yolks, 1½ teaspoons salt, and dash pepper.

Stir in cooked mushrooms and parsley. Spoon into greased 2-quart casserole. Melt remaining 2 tablespoons butter; toss with soft bread crumbs. Sprinkle atop potatoes. Cover and refrigerate. Bake, uncovered, at 350° till hot, 45 to 50 minutes. (If casserole is not chilled, bake, uncovered, for 25 to 30 minutes.) Makes 8 servings.

Marinated Asparagus Salad

2 9-ounce packages frozen asparagus
    spears or 2 pounds fresh asparagus
    spears
1 cup oil and vinegar salad dressing
    with seasonings
¼ cup finely chopped dill pickle
¼ cup finely chopped green pepper
2 tablespoons snipped parsley
2 tablespoons drained capers
2 hard-cooked eggs
  Lettuce
  Canned pimiento slices

Cook spears in boiling salted water till tender; drain. In screw-top jar combine dressing, pickle, green pepper, parsley, and capers. Cover; shake well. Dice *one* of the eggs; stir into dressing. Pour over spears in shallow dish. Chill thoroughly.

To serve, arrange asparagus on lettuce-lined platter; spoon dressing over. Cut remaining egg into wedges; use as garnish with pimiento. Makes 8 servings.

TV Buffet

Serves 6

Beef-Broccoli Pie
Cottage-Apricot Ring   Tomatoes
Whole Wheat Bread   Butter
Lime Sherbet
Milk   Coffee

BUFFET SERVING TIP: When you invite friends over to watch television and eat, use TV trays so all can view easily. Be sure to allow ample room around trays.

Beef-Broccoli Pie

> **Meat-Broccoli Filling**
> **2 packages refrigerated crescent rolls**
> **4 ounces Monterey Jack cheese**

Prepare Meat-Broccoli Filling; keep warm. Unroll *one* package of rolls. On floured surface place 4 sections of dough together in a 12x7-inch rectangle. Seal edges and perforations. Roll into a 12-inch square. Fit into 9-inch pie plate; trim. Fill with meat-broccoli mixture. Slice cheese; place on top of meat. Roll remaining rolls into a 12-inch square as before. Place atop meat. Trim; seal edges. Cut slits in top; brush with milk, if desired. Bake at 350° for 40 minutes. If pie browns too quickly, cover with foil last 20 minutes. Let stand 10 minutes before serving. Makes 6 servings.

Meat-Broccoli Filling: Cook one 10-ounce package frozen chopped broccoli according to package directions. Drain well; set aside. Brown 1 pound ground beef and ¼ cup chopped onion; drain off fat. Stir 2 tablespoons all-purpose flour, ¾ teaspoon salt, and ¼ teaspoon garlic salt into beef. Add 1¼ cups milk and one 3-ounce package cream cheese, softened. Cook and stir till thick and smooth. Add moderate amount of hot mixture to 1 beaten egg; return to meat mixture. Cook and stir till thick. Stir in broccoli.

Cottage-Apricot Ring

A cool, apricot-flavored dinner salad—

> **½ cup sugar**
> **2 envelopes unflavored gelatin**
> **¼ teaspoon salt**
> **1½ cups water**
> **1 17-ounce can apricot halves**
> **¼ cup lemon juice**
> **Few drops yellow food coloring**
> **1½ cups cream-style cottage cheese, undrained**
> **Lettuce**

In saucepan combine sugar, unflavored gelatin, and salt. Add 1½ cups water; heat and stir till gelatin dissolves. Drain apricot halves, reserving syrup. Add enough water to reserved syrup to make 1½ cups liquid. Add syrup mixture, lemon juice, and few drops yellow food coloring to gelatin mixture. Chill mixture till partially set.

Cut up apricot halves. Fold undrained cottage cheese and apricots into partially set gelatin mixture. Pour into 5½- or 6-cup mold. Chill till firm. Unmold on lettuce-lined platter. Makes 6 servings.

To prepare a meat piecrust from crescent roll dough, carefully seal edges and perforations by pinching dough together with fingers.

Weekday Buffet
Serves 10

Meat Loaf-Potato Roll-Up
Buttered Carrot Circles
Curried Pea Salad
or
Waldorf Salad
Fantan Rolls   Butter
Choco-Brickle Squares
Milk   Coffee

BUFFET SERVING TIP: To simplify serving meat loaf, slice before placing on the buffet. Serve catsup warm in a heatproof container over a candle or on a warming tray.

Meat Loaf-Potato Roll-Up

    4 beaten eggs
    1 cup crushed saltine crackers
        (28 crackers)
    ⅔ cup tomato sauce
    ½ cup finely chopped onion
    ¼ cup chopped green pepper
    1½ teaspoons salt
    3 pounds ground beef
      Packaged instant mashed potatoes
        (enough for 6 servings)
    1 cup shredded sharp Cheddar cheese
    2 tablespoons snipped parsley
    ¼ teaspoon dried thyme, crushed
    ¼ teaspoon dried marjoram, crushed
      Warmed catsup

Combine first 6 ingredients; add meat and mix well. Divide in half. Pat each portion on waxed paper into a 10x8-inch rectangle; set aside. Prepare potatoes according to package directions; stir in cheese, parsley, thyme, and marjoram. Spoon half of potatoes down center of each meat rectangle. Fold sides of meat over potato; seal. Place rolls side by side, seam side down, on 15½x10½x1-inch baking pan. Bake at 350° about 45 minutes. Serve with warmed catsup. Serves 10.

Curried Pea Salad
A quick salad that doubles as a relish—

    ⅔ cup vinegar
    ½ cup sugar
    ½ cup salad oil
    2 tablespoons chopped canned pimiento
    2 teaspoons curry powder
    ¼ teaspoon pepper
            • • •
    2 10-ounce packages frozen peas, cooked
        and drained
    2 small onions, sliced and separated
        into rings
    ⅔ cup chopped celery
      Lettuce cups

In screw-top jar combine vinegar, sugar, oil, chopped pimiento, curry, and pepper; cover and shake well. Combine peas, onion rings, and celery in medium bowl; pour dressing over vegetables. Cover and refrigerate 8 hours or overnight. Stir once or twice. To serve, drain vegetables and spoon into lettuce cups. Makes 10 servings.

Choco-Brickle Squares
Store extra dessert in the freezer for snacks—

    ¼ cup butter or margarine
    ¼ cup packed brown sugar
    1½ cups wheat germ
    ⅓ cup chopped walnuts
    1 quart butter brickle ice cream,
        softened
    1 pint chocolate ice cream, softened

In saucepan melt butter or margarine. Stir in brown sugar; cook over medium heat till bubbly. Stir in wheat germ and chopped walnuts; mix well. Remove from heat.

Set aside *1 cup* of the wheat germ mixture. Press remaining mixture evenly into bottom of 9x9x2-inch baking pan; chill. Spread *half* of the softened butter brickle ice cream over crust. Top with chocolate ice cream and then the remaining butter brickle ice cream. Sprinkle with reserved wheat germ mixture. Cover pan with clear plastic wrap or foil. Freeze till ice cream is firm. Cut in squares to serve. Makes 12 servings.

Weekend Buffet
Serves 12

Ham en Croustade
Creamed Potatoes   Green Beans
Cranberry Salad
Parkerhouse Rolls   Butter
Fruit Dip Medley
Milk   Coffee

BUFFET SERVING TIP: Carve the ham at the buffet table as friends fill their plates. After a leisurely dinner and good conversation, serve dessert from the coffee table.

Ham en Croustade

   1 5-pound canned ham (unglazed)
1½ cups all-purpose flour
   2 teaspoons baking powder
   ½ teaspoon rubbed sage
   ¼ teaspoon dry mustard
   3 tablespoons shortening
   ½ cup milk
   1 teaspoon caraway seed
   1 tablespoon prepared mustard
   2 tablespoons milk

Place ham on rack in shallow baking pan; bake at 325° till meat thermometer in center registers 135°, 1½ to 2 hours.

Meanwhile, thoroughly stir together flour, baking powder, sage, and dry mustard. Cut in shortening till size of coarse crumbs. Add ½ cup milk and caraway; stir till dough follows fork around bowl. Turn out on floured surface. Knead gently 12 strokes. Roll into a 12-inch square, ¼ inch thick. Remove ham from oven; increase oven temperature to 450°. Remove rack; discard drippings. Brush top and sides of ham with prepared mustard. Drape pastry over ham; mold to surface. Trim. Make slits in top. Make cutouts from remaining dough; arrange on loaf. Brush with 2 tablespoons milk. Bake at 450° till browned, about 10 minutes. Makes 12 servings.

Fruit Dip Medley

   ½ cup maraschino cherry syrup
   1 tablespoon cornstarch
   ¼ cup finely chopped maraschino
      cherries
   ¼ teaspoon shredded lemon peel
   1 cup dairy sour cream
   1 small pineapple, peeled, eyes removed,
      cored, and cut into chunks
   1 pint whole strawberries
   1 bunch seedless green grapes

In saucepan gradually stir cherry syrup into cornstarch. Cook and stir over medium heat till thick and bubbly; cook and stir 2 minutes longer. Remove from heat; stir in cherries and lemon peel. Cool slightly. Stir into sour cream. Chill thoroughly.

To serve, place dip in bowl in center of large serving tray; arrange fruits around edge of tray. Serve with cocktail picks for dipping. Makes 1⅓ cups dip.

Gently drape pastry over baked ham. With fingers, mold and shape dough over top and sides of meat to completely cover exposed surfaces.

Buffet for the Gang

Serves 24 (halve for 12)

Curry-Sauced Ham
Quantity Oven Rice
Pineapple-Pear Mold
Assorted Relishes
Parmesan-Parsley Bread
German Chocolate Cake
Coffee

BUFFET SERVING TIP: If space and equipment are available, arrange the table for a two-line buffet. However, if this is not possible, keep an eye on serving dishes and replace as needed so table always looks ample.

Curry-Sauced Ham

    3 10-ounce packages frozen mixed
        vegetables
    1½ cups chopped celery
    1½ cups chopped onion
    1 cup water
    4 10¾-ounce cans condensed cream of
        mushroom soup
    2 10½-ounce cans condensed cream of
        potato soup
    3 to 4 tablespoons curry powder
    4 cups milk
    12 cups cubed fully cooked ham
        (about 4 pounds)
    ⅔ cup all-purpose flour
    2 cups dairy sour cream

In large Dutch oven combine mixed vegetables, celery, onion, and water; bring to a boil. Reduce heat; simmer, covered, for 10 minutes. Stir in soups and curry. Gradually add milk; stir in ham. Simmer, covered, for 20 minutes. Slowly stir flour into sour cream. Add to ham mixture; cook and stir till thickened (*do not boil*). Serve over Quantity Oven Rice. Serves 24.
To serve 12: Use half recipe, *except* use two 10-ounce packages frozen mixed vegetables.

Pineapple-Pear Mold

    2 13¼-ounce cans pineapple tidbits
    1 29-ounce can pear slices
    2 6-ounce packages lemon-flavored
        gelatin
    3 cups cold water
    1 6-ounce can frozen limeade
        concentrate, thawed
    Several drops green food coloring
    Lettuce

Drain pineapple and pears; reserve syrups. Add enough water to syrups to make 4 cups. In large saucepan heat syrup mixture to boiling; remove from heat. Add gelatin; stir till dissolved. Stir in 3 cups cold water, limeade concentrate, and food coloring; chill till partially set.

Fold in pineapple and pears. Divide and pour into two 6- or 6½-cup molds. Chill till firm. To serve, unmold on two lettuce-lined platters. Makes 24 servings.

Parmesan-Parsley Bread

    1 cup butter or margarine, softened
    ⅔ cup grated Parmesan cheese
    ⅓ cup snipped parsley
    2 tablespoons prepared horseradish
    ½ teaspoon celery salt
    2 loaves French bread, cut in 1-inch
        slices

Blend together butter, Parmesan, parsley, horseradish, and celery salt; let stand at room temperature for 1 hour. Spread one side of each bread slice with butter mixture; reassemble slices into loaves. Wrap each loaf loosely in foil; heat at 350° till hot through, 15 to 20 minutes.

Quantity Oven Rice

Place 2 cups long grain rice in *each* of two 2-quart casseroles. Add 2 teaspoons salt and 5 cups water to *each* casserole. Cover; bake at 350° for 30 minutes. Fluff with fork. Cover; continue baking till tender, 20 to 30 minutes more. Makes 24 servings.

Seafood Buffet

Serves 8

Salmon-Crab Veronique
Baked Patty Shells
Lemon Broccoli
Mushroom-Spinach Toss
Watermelon Pickles
Pineapple Sherbet   Date Drops
White Wine   Coffee

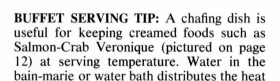

BUFFET SERVING TIP: A chafing dish is useful for keeping creamed foods such as Salmon-Crab Veronique (pictured on page 12) at serving temperature. Water in the bain-marie or water bath distributes the heat under the blazer pan containing the food.

Salmon-Crab Veronique

    6 tablespoons butter or margarine
    ¼ cup all-purpose flour
    1½ cups milk
    1½ cups light cream
    ⅓ cup dry white wine
    1 tablespoon lemon juice
    ½ teaspoon salt
    1 7¾-ounce can red salmon, drained
        and broken into large pieces
    1 7½-ounce can crab meat, drained,
        broken into large pieces, and
        cartilage removed
    1 cup halved and seeded Tokay or
        green grapes
    2 tablespoons snipped parsley
    8 frozen patty shells, baked

In blazer pan of chafing dish or saucepan melt butter over direct heat; blend in flour. Add milk and cream all at once; cook, stirring constantly, till thickened and bubbly. Cook and stir 2 to 3 minutes more. Blend in wine, lemon juice, and salt. Add salmon, crab, grapes, and parsley; heat through. Keep warm over hot water (bain-marie). Serve in patty shells. Makes 8 servings.

Lemon Broccoli

Cook three 10-ounce packages frozen broccoli spears according to package directions; drain well in colander. In small saucepan cook ½ cup chopped green onion and ½ cup chopped celery in 6 tablespoons butter or margarine till tender but not brown. Stir in 2 tablespoons lemon juice; heat through. To serve, layer broccoli and butter sauce in a serving dish. Sprinkle with ½ teaspoon shredded lemon peel. Makes 8 servings.

Mushroom-Spinach Toss

Pour ½ cup Italian salad dressing over 2 cups sliced fresh mushrooms; cover. Chill 3 hours. Drain; reserve dressing. Combine 3 cups torn fresh spinach, 3 cups torn romaine, ¾ cup sliced radishes, 2 tablespoons crumbled blue cheese, and mushrooms. Toss with reserved dressing. Serves 8.

Date Drops

    1 cup finely chopped pitted dates
    ½ cup packed brown sugar
    ½ cup butter or margarine
    ¼ cup milk
    1 egg
    1½ cups all-purpose flour
    ½ teaspoon salt
    ½ teaspoon baking powder
    ¼ teaspoon baking soda
    ½ cup chopped nuts
    Frosting

Combine dates and ½ cup water; bring to a boil. Simmer 5 minutes; cool. Set aside *2 tablespoons* date mixture for frosting. To remaining dates beat in sugar, butter, milk, and egg. Stir together flour, salt, baking powder, and soda. Add to egg mixture; stir in nuts. Drop from teaspoon onto ungreased cookie sheet. Bake at 375° for 10 to 12 minutes. Cool; spread with Frosting. Makes 36.

Frosting: Beat together 3 tablespoons butter, softened; 1½ cups sifted powdered sugar; ½ teaspoon vanilla; and reserved dates. Add enough milk to make spreadable.

Block Party Buffet

Serves 24 (halve for 12)

Antipasto Roll-Ups
Cheese Spread   Crackers
Seafood-Noodle Bake
Fried Chicken
Scalloped Corn
Grilled Tomatoes
Caesar Buffet Salad
Dinner Rolls   Butter
Watermelon
Soft Drinks   Iced Tea

BUFFET SERVING TIP: Invite neighbors to help plan and prepare a summertime block buffet. For easier access to food and less confusion, use individual tables for serving appetizers, main course, dessert, and beverage.

Caesar Buffet Salad

Keep extra salads crisp in the refrigerator till needed, then toss with dressing and serve —

1½ cups salad oil
½ cup red wine vinegar
¼ cup lemon juice
3 cloves garlic, crushed
   Dash freshly ground pepper
2 2-ounce cans anchovy fillets, drained
4 medium heads romaine, chilled
½ cup grated Parmesan cheese
4 cups cheese and garlic croutons
2 eggs

In screw-top jar combine oil, vinegar, lemon juice, garlic, and pepper; cover and shake well. Chop *half* the anchovies; add to dressing. Cover; chill several hours or overnight. Into 3 or 4 large salad bowls tear romaine into bite-size pieces. Sprinkle Parmesan and croutons among salad bowls. Add eggs to dressing; shake well. (Refrigerate if not used immediately.) Before serving, toss dressing with salad. Garnish with remaining anchovies. Serves 24.

Antipasto Roll-Ups

1 6½- or 7-ounce can tuna, drained
1 hard-cooked egg, chopped
¼ cup mayonnaise or salad dressing
1 teaspoon lemon juice
2 6-ounce packages sliced mozzarella
   cheese
2 8-ounce packages sliced party salami

Flake tuna; mash with next 3 ingredients. Set aside. Cut each cheese slice into quarters. Place one quarter on *each* slice salami; trim to fit. Spread about *1 teaspoon* tuna mixture over cheese. Roll up; secure with 3 wooden picks. Chill. To serve, cut each roll into thirds. Makes 96.

Seafood-Noodle Bake

2 cups chopped onion
½ cup butter or margarine
2 10¾-ounce cans condensed cream of
   mushroom soup
2 10½-ounce cans condensed cream of
   shrimp soup
2 cups milk
2 cups shredded sharp American
   cheese (8 ounces)
3 7½-ounce cans crab meat, drained,
   flaked, and cartilage removed
3 4½-ounce cans shrimp, drained
2 6-ounce cans sliced mushrooms,
   drained
⅓ cup snipped parsley
16 ounces noodles, cooked and drained
3 cups soft bread crumbs

In Dutch oven cook onion in *6 tablespoons* of the butter till tender; add soups and milk. Heat and stir till smooth; add cheese. Stir till melted. Remove from heat; stir in crab, shrimp, mushrooms, and parsley.

Divide noodles between two 13x9x2-inch baking dishes; spoon *half* of seafood mixture into each. Mix gently. Melt remaining butter; toss with crumbs. Sprinkle over casseroles. Bake, uncovered, at 350° till hot through, 35 to 45 minutes. Serves 24.

To serve 12: Make half recipe, using 3 cans seafood. Bake in 13x9x2-inch baking dish.

Late-Night Suppers

Steak Supper

Serves 6

Peppered Steak Diane
Lemon Rice
Spicy Italian Salad
Butterhorn Rolls   Butter
Apple Turnovers
Burgundy   Coffee

BUFFET SERVING TIP: Serve steak strips in a handsome chafing dish or a colorful electric skillet to make certain they remain hot on the buffet table. To keep rice warm, serve it in a bowl or attractive saucepan placed on a warming tray or over a candle.

Spicy Italian Salad

½ cup salad oil
⅓ cup tarragon vinegar
1 tablespoon sugar
1 teaspoon dried thyme, crushed
½ teaspoon dry mustard
1 small clove garlic, minced
1 7-ounce can artichoke hearts, drained and halved
3 cups torn romaine
3 cups torn lettuce
1 small green pepper, cut in strips
½ cup chopped summer sausage
¼ cup sliced pitted ripe olives
2 tablespoons grated Parmesan cheese

In screw-top jar combine first 6 ingredients. Cover; shake well. Pour over artichoke hearts. Cover; marinate in refrigerator 4 to 6 hours or overnight.

In salad bowl combine remaining ingredients; add artichokes with the dressing mixture. Toss. Makes 6 servings.

Peppered Steak Diane

1½ pounds beef sirloin steak, cut 1 inch thick
½ teaspoon salt
⅛ teaspoon freshly ground black pepper
¼ cup butter or margarine
¼ teaspoon dry mustard
1 3-ounce can sliced mushrooms, drained
3 tablespoons dry white wine
1 tablespoon lemon juice
2 teaspoons snipped chives
1 teaspoon Worcestershire sauce
¼ cup cold water
1 tablespoon all-purpose flour
Lemon Rice

Cut steak in ¼-inch-wide strips. Sprinkle with salt and freshly ground pepper. In skillet or chafing dish melt butter or margarine. Brown the meat strips in hot butter. Stir in dry mustard. Add mushrooms, wine, lemon juice, chives, and Worcestershire sauce.

Blend cold water into flour; stir into meat mixture. Cook, stirring constantly, till thickened and bubbly. Garnish with lemon slice and watercress, if desired. Serve over Lemon Rice. Makes 6 servings.

Lemon Rice

In saucepan over medium-low heat melt ¼ cup butter. Add 2 teaspoons ground turmeric, 1 teaspoon salt, and 1 teaspoon mustard seed. Cook 5 minutes. Stir in 3 cups cooked long grain rice (1 cup uncooked); heat through. Mix in 3 tablespoons lemon juice. Serves 6.

Buffet for steak lovers

Let friends help themselves to *Peppered Steak →
Diane,* a new version of a gourmet classic. Serve wine-sauced steak strips over *Lemon Rice;* accompany with a crisp salad and hot rolls.

Candlelight Supper

Serves 6 (double for 12)

Swiss Veal
Mixed Greens   Italian Dressing
Herb Twists   Butter
Lime Sherbet with Crème de Menthe
White Wine   Coffee

BUFFET SERVING TIP: Set the mood for the evening with soft-glowing candlelight. Select candles of varying sizes, shapes, and colors to illuminate the dining area. For an eye-catching centerpiece, arrange several candles on a silver tray or mirror and place on the buffet table.

Herb Twists

Bake, then reduce oven heat for Swiss Veal

1 13¾-ounce package hot roll mix
1 teaspoon rubbed sage
½ teaspoon dried basil, crushed
2 tablespoons butter, melted

Prepare hot roll mix according to package directions, *except* add sage and basil to the dry mix. Turn out on lightly floured surface; knead till smooth, 2 to 3 minutes. Place dough in greased bowl, turning once to grease surface. Cover; let rise in warm place till double (about 45 minutes). Punch down. Cover; let rest 10 minutes. Turn dough out on lightly floured board. Roll dough to an 18x8-inch rectangle.

Brush *half* of dough, lengthwise, with the melted butter. Fold the unbuttered half over the buttered portion, pressing gently, to make 18x4-inch rectangle.

Slice dough crosswise into 1-inch-wide strips. Holding strips by ends, twist several times; place on lightly greased baking sheet. Let rise in warm place for 20 minutes. Bake rolls at 425° till golden brown, 8 to 10 minutes. Cool rolls slightly on rack before serving. Makes 18 rolls.

Swiss Veal

1½ pounds veal round steak
2 beaten eggs
1 cup fine dry bread crumbs
2 tablespoons cooking oil
1 15-ounce can stroganoff sauce
1 large avocado, cut in 6 wedges
1 large tomato, cut in 6 wedges
¾ cup shredded Swiss cheese or 6 slices Swiss cheese (3 ounces)

Cut veal in 6 pieces; pound very thin with meat mallet. Dip in eggs, then in crumbs. Brown on both sides in hot oil, about 5 minutes. Place in 13x9x2-inch baking dish. Heat sauce; pour over veal. Place *one* avocado wedge and *one* tomato wedge atop *each* piece of veal. Cover with cheese. Bake at 350° till bubbly, 5 to 7 minutes. Serves 6. *To serve 12:* Bake in two 13x9x2-inch baking dishes till cheese melts and sauce bubbles.

To give a fresh-from-the-bakery look to *Herb Twists,* hold dough strips by ends and twist several times. Then place on baking sheet.

Soup Supper

Serves 12

Marinated Tidbit Tray
Potage Elegante
Crisp Relishes
Cheese Buns   Butter
Plum Pudding   Hard Sauce
Tea   Coffee

BUFFET SERVING TIP: Ask friends to join you on a cold winter night for a soup buffet in front of a blazing fire. Be sure to provide large soup bowls with liners to catch any accidental spills. If table space is limited, let guests eat from trays.

Marinated Tidbit Tray

   **2 9-ounce packages frozen artichoke
     hearts
   2 10-ounce packages frozen cauliflower
   2 cups cleaned cooked shrimp**
       • • •
   **3 cups salad oil
   1 cup white wine vinegar
   2 tablespoons sugar
   2 tablespoons lemon juice
   3 cloves garlic, minced
   2 teaspoons salt
   ½ teaspoon dry mustard
   ¼ teaspoon white pepper
   ¼ teaspoon cayenne**

Cook artichokes and cauliflower according to package directions; drain. Place artichokes, cauliflower, and cooked shrimp in large plastic bag or deep bowl.

In screw-top jar combine oil, vinegar, sugar, lemon juice, garlic, salt, dry mustard, white pepper, and cayenne; cover and shake well. Pour over vegetables and shrimp. Chill several hours; stir occasionally. Drain; serve vegetables and shrimp in shallow bowl or deep platter. Garnish with parsley sprigs, if desired. Serves 12.

Potage Elegante

Prepare stock and vegetables 1 or 2 days ahead—

   **2½ to 3 pounds cracked beef soup bones
   3 medium potatoes, peeled and cut in
     large pieces (about 3 cups)
   3 medium carrots, coarsely chopped
   2 medium turnips, peeled and coarsely
     chopped
   2 medium onions, quartered
   ½ cup snipped parsley
   2 tablespoons butter or margarine
   1 cup light cream
   2 beaten egg yolks
     Grated Parmesan cheese**

Bake bones in shallow baking pan at 450° till browned, about 15 minutes. In large kettle cook vegetables and parsley in butter till lightly browned. Add bones, 3 quarts water, and 4 teaspoons salt. Cover; simmer 1 hour. Remove meat from bones; discard bones.

Strain soup; reserve stock and vegetables. In blender purée the vegetables. Combine stock, meat, and puréed vegetables. Boil gently till soup measures 2½ quarts. (Refrigerate 1 to 2 days, if desired.)

Heat soup. Combine cream and egg yolks. Stir *some* of the hot soup into cream mixture; return to soup. Cook till slightly thickened. Sprinkle with Parmesan cheese and additional parsley, if desired. Serves 12.

Cheese Buns

In mixing bowl combine 1 cup all-purpose flour and 1 package active dry yeast. Heat together one 5-ounce jar sharp American cheese spread, ½ cup water, ¼ cup shortening, 2 tablespoons sugar, and 1 teaspoon salt just till warm (115° to 120°); stir to melt shortening. Add to yeast mixture; add 1 egg. Beat at low speed of electric mixer for ½ minute; scrape bowl constantly. Beat 3 minutes at high speed.

By hand, stir in 1 cup all-purpose flour. (If smoother surface is desired, knead dough lightly.) Shape into 12 rolls; place in well-greased muffin pans. Let rise in warm place till nearly double, 1 to 1½ hours. Bake at 350° for 15 to 18 minutes. Makes 12.

Casserole Supper

Serves 8

Chicken and Rice Casserole
Mediterranean Salad
Spiced Peaches
Strawberries Romanoff
Coffee

BUFFET SERVING TIP: Casseroles make great buffet fare, because they're easy to serve and often eliminate the need for several separate dishes. To keep a casserole warm, place it on a warming tray.

Mediterranean Salad

2 tablespoons butter or margarine
3 slices bread, cut in cubes (2 cups)
1 12-ounce can whole kernel corn, drained
1 9-ounce package frozen Italian green beans, cooked and drained
½ cup mayonnaise or salad dressing
2 tablespoons chopped canned pimiento
1 teaspoon dried basil, crushed
¼ teaspoon salt

In skillet melt butter; add bread cubes. Cook till crisp, turning occasionally. Combine corn, beans, mayonnaise, pimiento, basil, and salt; chill. Before serving, toss bread cubes with salad. Serves 8.

Spiced Peaches

Drain one 29-ounce can peach halves, reserving syrup. Set peaches aside. In small saucepan combine reserved syrup, ¼ cup sugar, 1 tablespoon vinegar, 6 inches stick cinnamon, and ½ teaspoon whole cloves. Simmer, uncovered, 5 minutes. Add peaches; heat through. Cool. Stir in ¼ cup brandy (optional). Chill peaches in covered container at least 48 hours before serving.

Chicken and Rice Casserole

½ cup wild rice
½ cup long grain rice
½ cup chopped onion
½ cup butter or margarine
¼ cup all-purpose flour
• • •
1 6-ounce can sliced mushrooms
Chicken broth
1½ cups light cream
3 cups diced cooked chicken
¼ cup chopped canned pimiento
¼ cup snipped parsley
1 teaspoon salt
Dash pepper
¼ cup toasted slivered almonds

Rinse wild rice in cold water. Add with ½ teaspoon salt to 2 cups boiling water. Cook 20 minutes. Add long grain rice, 1 cup boiling water, and ½ teaspoon salt; cook 20 minutes longer. Meanwhile, cook chopped onion in butter or margarine till tender but not brown. Remove from heat; stir in flour.

Drain mushrooms, reserving liquid. Add enough chicken broth to liquid to measure 1½ cups. Stir into flour mixture. Add cream. Cook and stir till thickened and bubbly. Add rice, mushrooms, chicken, pimiento, parsley, 1 teaspoon salt, and dash pepper. Turn into 2-quart casserole. Top with almonds. Bake at 350° for 25 to 30 minutes. Serves 8.

Strawberries Romanoff

3 pints whole strawberries, sliced
⅔ cup orange liqueur
¼ cup sugar
• • •
1 cup whipping cream
¼ cup sugar
2 teaspoons vanilla
Shredded orange peel

Combine strawberries, liqueur, and ¼ cup sugar; chill at least 2 hours. Whip cream with ¼ cup sugar and vanilla till soft peaks form. Spoon berries and liquid into sherbet dishes; top with whipped cream. Garnish with shredded orange peel. Makes 8 servings.

Around-the-World Supper
Serves 6

Ratatouille
Veal Burgers Scallopini
Bulgur Wheat Pilaf
Flan
White Wine
Espresso Coffee

BUFFET SERVING TIP: Carry the international mood into the evening by serving espresso coffee in the living room after supper. Serve it in demitasse cups with a lemon twist. For those who want cream, top the espresso with whipped cream.

Bulgur Wheat Pilaf

In saucepan melt 2 tablespoons butter or margarine. Add ¾ cup bulgur wheat and 2 tablespoons chopped onion; brown lightly, stirring often. Add 2 cups beef *or* chicken broth and dash pepper. Bring to boiling. Cover; reduce heat and simmer till done, about 20 minutes. Season with salt and pepper. Makes 6 servings.

Flan

In 8-inch skillet caramelize ⅓ cup sugar by heating and stirring it over medium heat till melted and golden brown. Quickly pour into 8x1½-inch round baking dish; tilt dish to spread sugar over entire bottom.

In blender container put two 13-ounce cans evaporated milk, 4 eggs, 2 teaspoons vanilla, and ½ cup sugar. Adjust lid; blend to combine. Pour mixture into baking dish; set in shallow pan on oven rack. Pour hot water into pan, 1 inch deep. Bake at 325° till knife inserted off-center comes out clean, about 45 minutes. (Center will be soft.) Chill. Before serving, carefully loosen sides; invert on platter. Makes 8 servings.

Ratatouille

1¾ cups coarsely chopped onion
1 clove garlic, minced
2 tablespoons cooking oil
4 medium tomatoes, coarsely chopped
½ pound eggplant, cut in ½-inch strips
½ pound zucchini, cut in strips
2 green peppers, cut in strips
1 teaspoon salt
2 or 3 fresh basil leaves, snipped, *or*
    1 teaspoon dried basil, crushed
2 sprigs fresh thyme, snipped, *or*
    ½ teaspoon dried thyme, crushed
Dash freshly ground pepper

In large skillet cook onion and garlic in oil till tender but not brown. Add remaining ingredients. Cover; bring to boiling. Reduce heat; simmer 40 minutes. Stir occasionally; avoid breaking up vegetables. Chill. Serve as an hors d'oeuvre. (Or, heat and serve as a side dish.) Serves 6 to 8.

Veal Burgers Scallopini

1 beaten egg
2 tablespoons milk
1 cup soft bread crumbs
    (about 1½ slices)
½ teaspoon salt
Dash pepper
1½ pounds ground veal
¼ cup all-purpose flour
¼ cup shortening
• • •
1 8-ounce can tomato sauce
1 3-ounce can chopped mushrooms
¼ cup white wine
1 tablespoon finely snipped parsley
¼ teaspoon dried oregano, crushed
Grated Parmesan cheese

Combine egg, milk, crumbs, salt, and pepper. Add veal; mix well. Shape into 6 patties; coat with flour. In skillet brown the patties in hot shortening; drain. Combine tomato sauce, undrained mushrooms, wine, parsley, and oregano; pour over meat. Cover; simmer 20 to 25 minutes. Before serving, sprinkle with Parmesan cheese. Makes 6 servings.

Margarita Cocktail

Mix drinks individually to order —

⅔ **jigger tequila (1 ounce)**
Dash Triple Sec
Juice of ½ lime
½ **cup crushed or cracked ice**

Put all ingredients in blender container; blend. Strain into salt-rimmed cocktail glass prepared by rubbing glass rim with cut lime and dipping in salt. Makes 1 drink.

Avocado Dip

Combine 2 cups dairy sour cream; 1 avocado, peeled, pitted, and finely chopped; 1 tomato, peeled and chopped; 1 envelope onion soup mix; and 1 teaspoon ground cumin. Chill. Serve with corn chips. Makes 3 cups.

Corn Tortillas

For easy shaping, use a tortilla press. They are usually available at specialty food stores —

2 cups corn flour (masa harina)
1 cup water

In medium mixing bowl combine corn flour and water; mix well with hands. Add more water to dough, if needed. (Dough should be moist, but it will hold its shape.)

Divide dough into 12 balls. Dampen balls slightly with water; press balls between sheets of waxed paper, using a tortilla press or a flat baking dish. Gently peel off top sheet of waxed paper from tortilla.

Place tortilla, paper side up, on hot, ungreased griddle. Gently peel off remaining piece of paper. Cook tortilla till edges begin to dry, about 30 seconds. Turn; cook till puffs appear. Makes 12.

Journey south-of-the-border with friends for a Mexican buffet served in your own home. Watch hot pepper fans relish *Green Enchiladas* with *Spicy Sauce*. For diners with timid palates, use mild peppers.

Mexican Fiesta
Serves 6

Avocado Dip   Corn Chips
Margarita Cocktails
Green Enchiladas   Spicy Sauce
Mexican Frijoles Salad
Cantaloupe Wedges
Coffee

BUFFET SERVING TIP: Add a touch of Old Mexico to the buffet with gaily colored paper flowers arranged in straw baskets around the dining area. Hang castanets and a large Mexican straw hat on the wall behind the buffet. For table runners, trim vividly colored felt strips with ball fringe.

Mexican Frijoles Salad

> 2 tablespoons salad oil
> 2 tablespoons vinegar
> 1 small clove garlic, minced
> ½ teaspoon chili powder
>   Dash pepper
> 1 16-ounce can pinto beans, drained
> 1 16-ounce can red kidney beans, drained
> ¾ cup diced celery
> ¼ cup small white onion rings
> 2 tablespoons sweet pickle relish
>   Lettuce
>   Onion rings (optional)

In mixing bowl combine oil, vinegar, garlic, chili powder, and pepper; beat thoroughly with rotary beater. Set aside.

In second bowl combine pinto beans, kidney beans, celery, ¼ cup onion rings, and pickle relish. Pour marinade over bean mixture; toss lightly. Cover; chill several hours or overnight, stirring occasionally.

To serve, spoon bean mixture into large lettuce-lined bowl or individual salad bowls. Garnish with additional onion rings, if desired. Makes 6 to 8 servings.

Green Enchiladas
Use homemade, canned, or frozen tortillas —

> 12 corn tortillas
> ½ cup cooking oil
> 2 cups shredded Monterey Jack cheese (8 ounces)
> ¾ cup chopped onion
>   • • •
> ¼ cup butter or margarine
> ¼ cup all-purpose flour
> 2 cups chicken broth
> 1 cup dairy sour cream
> 1 4-ounce can jalapeño peppers, seeded and chopped
>   • • •
>   Spicy Sauce

In skillet cook tortillas, one at a time, in hot oil for 15 seconds on each side. (Do not overcook or they will not roll.) Drain. Place *2 tablespoons* shredded cheese and *1 tablespoon* onion on each tortilla; roll up. Place tortillas, seam side down, in 12x7½x2-inch baking dish.

In medium saucepan melt butter or margarine; blend in flour. Add chicken broth all at once; cook, stirring constantly, till mixture thickens and bubbles. Stir in sour cream and chopped peppers; cook mixture till heated through *but do not boil*. Pour sour cream sauce over rolled tortillas in baking dish. Bake at 425° for 20 minutes. Sprinkle remaining shredded Monterey Jack cheese atop tortillas; return to oven just till cheese melts, about 5 minutes more. Serve green enchiladas with Spicy Sauce. Serves 6.

Spicy Sauce
Select a milder pepper to reduce hotness —

> 1 medium tomato, finely chopped
> ½ cup finely chopped onion
> 2 jalapeño peppers including seeds, finely chopped
> ¼ cup tomato juice
> ½ teaspoon salt

In mixing bowl combine finely chopped tomato, onion, peppers, tomato juice, and salt. Serve with Green Enchiladas.

Continental Supper

Serves 6

Italian Beans Vinaigrette
Belgian Cheese Croquettes
Tomato Sauce
Mixed Greens   Garlic Dressing
Lemon Pound Cake
White Wine   Coffee

BUFFET SERVING TIP: It's easy to invite friends for a supper buffet after the concert or theater when a major portion of the menu is prepared earlier in the day. Let guests socialize over cocktails and hors d'oeuvres while you deep-fry croquettes, heat sauce, and toss the salad.

Italian Beans Vinaigrette

Prepare this novel appetizer in advance —

    2 9-ounce packages frozen Italian
       green beans
              • • •
    1 cup cooking oil
    ⅓ cup vinegar
    2 tablespoons snipped parsley
    2 tablespoons finely chopped onion
    2 teaspoons dried basil, crushed
    2 teaspoons dried chervil, crushed
    1 teaspoon salt
    6 peppercorns

In saucepan bring frozen Italian green beans to a boil in salted water. Reduce heat and simmer just till green beans are tender-crisp, about 1 minute; drain.

In screw-top jar combine cooking oil, vinegar, snipped parsley, finely chopped onion, dried basil, dried chervil, salt, and peppercorns; cover and shake well. Pour over warm beans in bowl. Cover; chill beans in refrigerator several hours or overnight, stirring once or twice.

To serve, drain Italian green beans and serve with cocktail picks. Makes 4 cups.

Belgian Cheese Croquettes

    ¼ cup butter or margarine
    ⅓ cup all-purpose flour
    1½ cups milk
       Dash white pepper
       Dash ground nutmeg
    3 beaten egg yolks
    4 cups shredded Swiss cheese
       (16 ounces)
    2 eggs
    ½ cup milk
    ½ cup all-purpose flour
    1 cup fine dry bread crumbs
       Fat for frying
       Tomato Sauce

In saucepan melt butter; blend in ⅓ cup flour. Add 1½ cups milk all at once; cook and stir till thick and bubbly. Add pepper and nutmeg. Stir a moderate amount of hot mixture into egg yolks. Return the mixture to saucepan; cook 10 minutes, stirring constantly.

Add shredded Swiss cheese, stirring till smooth. Spread mixture in greased 11x7x1½-inch baking pan. Chill till firm.

Before serving, cut cheese mixture into 12 portions. Beat together 2 eggs and ½ cup milk. Gently roll croquettes in ½ cup flour; dip in egg mixture, then roll in bread crumbs to coat. Fry croquettes in deep hot fat (375°) till golden brown and heated through, 2 to 3 minutes. Serve with Tomato Sauce. Makes 6 servings.

Tomato Sauce

    ⅓ cup diced onion
    1 slice bacon, diced
    1 tablespoon butter or margarine
    1 10½-ounce can condensed beef broth
    1½ slices white bread
    ½ cup tomato purée
    ¼ cup catsup
    2 tablespoons diced carrot

In saucepan cook onion and bacon in butter till tender. Stir in beef broth, bread, purée, catsup, and carrot. Cover; cook over low heat 30 minutes. Press through sieve; serve hot over croquettes. Makes 1¼ cups.

Midnight Supper

Serves 4

Bacon-Oyster Bites
Mushroom Newburg
Baked Patty Shells
Dill-Dressed Cabbage
Tomato Relish   Celery Sticks
Apricot Sundaes
Coffee

BUFFET SERVING TIP: Invite friends for an intimate late-night supper. To add elegance to the buffet, set the table with fine china, crystal, and silver; use candles to enhance the setting. Offer appetizers for nibbling while you are making final preparations. Serve the newburg in a chafing dish.

Mushroom Newburg

An elegant entrée for late-night dining—

> 1 pound whole fresh mushrooms
> 1 tablespoon all-purpose flour
> ¼ cup butter or margarine
> 1¼ cups light cream
> ¼ cup dry sherry
> ¼ teaspoon salt
> ⅛ teaspoon ground nutmeg
> 3 beaten egg yolks
> 4 frozen patty shells, baked

Wash mushrooms; remove stems and reserve. (Halve mushroom caps if quite large.) Coat mushroom stems and caps with flour; brown in butter or margarine till all moisture has evaporated, about 5 minutes.

Add cream, sherry, salt, and nutmeg; cook, uncovered, till heated through, about 2 minutes. Add a little of the hot mixture to egg yolks; stir into mushroom mixture. Cook, stirring constantly, till bubbly; cook 2 minutes longer. Transfer mixture to blazer pan of chafing dish; keep warm over hot water (bain-marie). Serve in baked patty shells. Makes 4 servings.

Bacon-Oyster Bites

> ½ cup herb-seasoned stuffing mix
> 1 5-ounce can oysters, drained and chopped
> ¼ cup water
> 8 slices bacon, partially cooked and halved

Combine stuffing mix, oysters, and water; shape into balls, using about 1 teaspoon mixture for each. Wrap a half slice bacon around each; secure with wooden picks. Place on rack in shallow baking pan. Bake at 350° for 25 to 30 minutes. Makes 16.

Dill-Dressed Cabbage

> ½ cup mayonnaise or salad dressing
> ¼ cup milk
> 3 tablespoons grated Parmesan cheese
> 1 tablespoon white wine vinegar
> ½ teaspoon dried dillweed
> ⅛ teaspoon garlic powder
> Dash salt
> 1 small head Chinese cabbage

Mix first 7 ingredients. Cut cabbage crosswise into thin slices. Place on individual salad plates. Top with dressing. Sprinkle with paprika, if desired. Serves 4.

Apricot Sundaes

> ⅓ cup light cream
> ¼ cup butter or margarine
> ¼ cup sugar
> Dash salt
> ⅔ cup apricot preserves
> ¼ cup slivered almonds, toasted
> 1 tablespoon lemon juice
> Vanilla ice cream

In small saucepan combine cream, butter, sugar, and salt. Bring mixture to a boil over medium heat; cook, stirring constantly, for 10 minutes. Remove from heat; stir in apricot preserves, almonds, and lemon juice. Serve warm over scoops of vanilla ice cream. Makes about 1½ cups topping.

Buffets for Festive Occasions

Need help in organizing large-group buffets to celebrate a family wedding, anniversary, retirement, holiday, or one of life's other landmarks? Then glance through this section for buffet menus, themes, and serving ideas to aid in planning either a full meal or assorted appetizing tidbits.

For less momentous but just as festive occasions, you'll find tips for turning the popular outdoor barbecue and picnic into no-fuss buffets. There is also buffet fare designed for sports fans who gather to savor their team's victory after the final whistle blows.

And, to make the buffets more versatile, directions for tailoring recipes to serve various-size groups are included with some menus.

From easy-to-reach shelves partygoers sample *Sesame-Cheddar Wafers, Shrimp Tartlets, Confetti Log, Cauliflower with Anchovy,* and *Sausage Nibbles. Red Bubble Punch* is nearby at this Appetizer Buffet (see page 62).

Buffets to Honor Special Guests

Open House Tea

Serves 50

Crab Tea Sandwiches
Sweet Orange Pinwheels
Deviled Peanuts   Mints
Rosé Glow Punch
Tea   Coffee

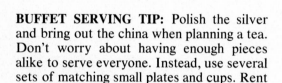

BUFFET SERVING TIP: Polish the silver and bring out the china when planning a tea. Don't worry about having enough pieces alike to serve everyone. Instead, use several sets of matching small plates and cups. Rent a punch bowl and cups, if desired. See page 11 for help in setting the tea table.

Quantity Tea

Tie 1 cup tea leaves loosely in cheesecloth bag. Place tea leaves *or* 40 individual tea bags in large kettle. Bring 9 quarts cold water to a boil; immediately pour over tea. Cover; steep 3 to 5 minutes. Remove tea; serve. Makes 50 (¾-cup) servings.

Quantity Egg Coffee

    2 slightly beaten eggs (reserve shells)
    2¼ to 2½ cups regular-grind coffee
    10 quarts cold water

In large kettle combine eggs, crumbled egg shells, and coffee. Pour in water. Bring to boiling; stir when foam starts to appear. Continue stirring till foam disappears. Remove from heat; let settle. If necessary, add 1 cup cold water to aid settling. Strain with fine mesh strainer or cloth before serving. Makes 50 (¾-cup) servings.

Rosé Glow Punch

    2 6-ounce cans frozen pink lemonade
        concentrate, thawed
    4 ⅘-quart bottles rosé wine, chilled
    1 cup brandy
    2 quarts ice cubes
    1 28-ounce bottle carbonated water,
        chilled

In punch bowl combine pink lemonade concentrate, wine, and brandy. Add ice cubes. Carefully add chilled carbonated water, pouring down side of punch bowl; stir mixture gently. Makes about 50 (4-ounce) servings.

Crab Tea Sandwiches

A delectable, open-face sandwich—

    4 hard-cooked eggs
    ½ cup mayonnaise or salad dressing
    ¼ cup cocktail sauce
    2 tablespoons lemon juice
    2 cups finely shredded lettuce
    ¾ cup finely chopped celery
    2 7½-ounce cans crab meat, drained,
        finely flaked, and cartilage
        removed
    14 slices sandwich-style white bread,
        toasted
    ½ cup butter or margarine, softened
        Paprika

Chop egg whites; set aside. Sieve egg yolks and set aside. Combine mayonnaise, cocktail sauce, and lemon juice. Stir in shredded lettuce, celery, chopped egg whites, and crab; mix well.

Spread toast with softened butter or margarine; trim edges. Cut each slice into quarters. Top each quarter with *1 heaping teaspoon* crab mixture. Sprinkle each with sieved yolk, then with paprika. (Sandwiches may be made ahead, covered with clear plastic wrap or foil, and refrigerated.) Makes 56 tea sandwiches.

Start in the center of this single-line tea table. After selecting *Crab Tea Sandwiches, Sweet Orange Pinwheels,* and *Deviled Nuts,* move to your left for tea or to your right for the *Rosé Glow Punch.*

Sweet Orange Pinwheels

Remove crusts from 1 loaf unsliced brown bread; cut into 6 *lengthwise* slices about ¾ inch thick. With rolling pin roll each slice to ⅛-inch thickness.

Blend together one 8-ounce package cream cheese, softened; ½ cup orange marmalade; and 2 tablespoons finely chopped candied ginger. Spread each bread slice with *2 tablespoons* cream cheese mixture.

Using ⅓ cup chopped walnuts, sprinkle about *1 tablespoon* nuts across *1* narrow end of *each* bread slice. Roll up jelly-roll style, beginning at nut-topped end. Wrap sandwich rolls in foil or clear plastic wrap; chill thoroughly. Before serving, slice into ⅜-inch pinwheels. Makes 50.

Deviled Peanuts

　　3 cups raw peanuts
　　2 tablespoons butter or margarine, melted
　　2 teaspoons chili powder
　1½ teaspoons onion salt
　　1 teaspoon celery salt
　　½ teaspoon garlic powder
　　⅛ teaspoon cayenne

Remove hulls from peanuts by rubbing between hands; set aside. In mixing bowl combine butter and remaining ingredients; add nuts. Stir to coat well. Spread in 13x9x2-inch baking pan. Roast at 350° till lightly browned, 25 to 30 minutes; shake pan occasionally. Makes 3 cups.

Get-Acquainted Coffee
Serves up to 30

Lemon-Filbert Bread
Buttery Cinnamon Cake
Date Dessert Crescents
Butter
Coffee

BUFFET SERVING TIP: Having a morning or afternoon coffee buffet is a convenient way to launch a big committee project. Let group size determine whether you prepare one, two, or all three of these goodies.

Buttery Cinnamon Cake

  1⅓ **cups granulated sugar**
  ⅔ **cup shortening**
  3 **eggs**
  ⅔ **cup milk**
  1½ **teaspoons vanilla**
  2 **cups all-purpose flour**
  1 **tablespoon baking powder**
  1 **teaspoon ground cinnamon**
  ¾ **teaspoon salt**
    Butter Syrup
    Sifted powdered sugar

In mixing bowl cream together granulated sugar and shortening. Add eggs, one at a time; beat well after each. Combine milk and vanilla. Thoroughly stir together flour, baking powder, cinnamon, and salt. Add to creamed mixture alternately with milk; beat well after each addition. Pour into well-greased 10-inch tube pan. Bake at 350° till done, about 40 minutes.

Remove hot cake from pan; prick with fork. Spoon hot Butter Syrup over hot cake. Cool. Sprinkle with sifted powdered sugar.

Butter Syrup: In saucepan combine ½ cup granulated sugar, 6 tablespoons butter or margarine, ⅓ cup water, 1 teaspoon vanilla, and ¾ teaspoon ground cinnamon. Heat and stir till butter melts; do not boil.

Lemon-Filbert Bread

Toast ½ cup chopped filberts in oven at 350° till lightly browned; cool. In mixing bowl stir together 2 cups all-purpose flour, ¾ cup sugar, 2 teaspoons baking powder, ½ teaspoon salt, and ¼ teaspoon baking soda. Mix 2 beaten eggs; ⅔ cup milk; ½ cup butter or margarine, melted; 2 teaspoons grated lemon peel; and ¼ cup lemon juice.

Stir egg-milk mixture into dry mixture just till all ingredients are moistened. Add toasted filberts. Pour into greased 9x5x3-inch loaf pan. Bake at 350° for 45 to 50 minutes. Remove from pan; cool. Wrap in foil; chill overnight. Slice. Makes 1 loaf.

Date Dessert Crescents

In a large mixing bowl stir together 3 cups all-purpose flour, one 3- or 3¼-ounce package *regular* vanilla pudding mix, and 1 package active dry yeast.

In a saucepan heat 2¼ cups milk, ½ cup butter or margarine, 2 teaspoons salt, and ½ teaspoon maple flavoring just till warm (115-120°), stirring constantly. Add warm milk mixture to flour mixture. Add 2 eggs. Beat at low speed of electric mixer ½ minute; scrape bowl constantly. Beat 3 minutes at high speed. By hand, stir in 3 to 3¼ cups all-purpose flour to form stiff dough. Place in lightly greased bowl. Cover; let rise in warm place till double (about 1 hour).

Divide into thirds. On floured surface roll each third into a 15-inch circle. Cut each circle into 12 pie-shaped wedges. Place *1 teaspoon* Filling on each wedge; roll up from wide end to point. Place, point down, on greased baking sheet. Curve to form crescent. Let rise in warm place till double (30 to 45 minutes). Bake at 375° for 12 to 15 minutes. Cool slightly; top with Icing. Makes 36.

Filling: Combine 1 cup finely snipped pitted dates, ⅓ cup water, and 2 tablespoons brown sugar; cook and stir over medium heat till thickened. Remove from heat; cool.

Icing: Combine 3 cups sifted powdered sugar, ¾ teaspoon maple flavoring, and enough milk to make icing of drizzling consistency (3 to 4 tablespoons).

Bridal Shower

Serves 24

Party Ham Pinwheels
Cucumber-Dill Sandwiches
Brandy Tarts
Spring Green Punch

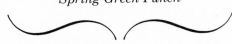

BUFFET SERVING TIP: Reinforce the theme of your shower with a clever centerpiece. For a kitchen shower, arrange flowers in a set of glass canisters; for a bath shower, use a soap-filled brandy snifter on the table.

Party Ham Pinwheels

Trim crusts from 1 loaf unsliced white bread; cut loaf into 5 *lengthwise* slices, ½ inch thick. Roll bread lightly with rolling pin. Spread with mixture of 3 tablespoons butter or margarine, softened, and 1½ teaspoons prepared horseradish. Place 10 thin slices boiled ham in single layer atop bread; trim, if needed, to fit. Spread one 5-ounce jar Neufchâtel cheese spread with pimientos over ham; sprinkle with 2 tablespoons finely chopped green onion tops. Roll up each slice jelly-roll style, beginning at narrow end. Wrap in foil or clear plastic wrap; chill. Slice into ⅜-inch pinwheels. Makes 45.

Cucumber-Dill Sandwiches

In mixing bowl blend one 8-ounce package cream cheese, softened, with 2 tablespoons milk till fluffy. Peel, seed, and finely chop 1 medium cucumber; add with ½ teaspoon dried dillweed to cheese mixture. Let stand at room temperature 2 hours.

Trim crusts from 1 loaf sliced pumpernickel bread. Using a variety of small cookie cutters, cut bread into assorted shapes. Spread bread cutouts with cheese mixture; garnish with snipped parsley. Cover loosely; chill till serving time. Makes 50 to 60.

Brandy Tarts

½ cup butter or margarine, softened
1 3-ounce package cream cheese, softened
1 cup all-purpose flour
1 3⅝- or 3¾-ounce package *instant* vanilla pudding mix
2 tablespoons white crème de cacao
2 tablespoons brandy
1 2-ounce package dessert topping mix
¼ cup chopped pecans *or* pistachio nuts

Blend together butter and cheese. Stir in flour. Chill 1½ hours. Shape into 2 dozen 1-inch balls; place in ungreased 1¾-inch miniature muffin pans. Press dough evenly against bottom and sides. Bake at 325° for 20 to 25 minutes. Cool; remove from pan.

Prepare pudding according to package directions, *except* use 1 cup milk. Stir in crème de cacao and brandy. Prepare topping according to package directions. Fold *1 cup* topping into pudding. (Chill remaining topping.) Chill till mixture mounds when spooned, 45 minutes. Spoon into tart shells; top with nuts. Chill. (Serve any remaining filling and topping as pudding.) Makes 24.

Spring Green Punch

3 6-ounce cans frozen limeade concentrate, thawed
1 6-ounce can frozen lemonade concentrate, thawed
1 cup sugar
2 envelopes unsweetened lemon-lime flavored soft drink mix
Few drops green food coloring
4 28-ounce bottles lemon-lime carbonated beverage, chilled

Combine concentrates, sugar, and soft drink mix; stir till all is dissolved. Stir in food coloring. Chill mixture thoroughly.

To serve, pour mixture into punch bowl; add 2 quarts cold water and ice. Slowly add carbonated beverage, pouring down side of bowl. Makes 50 (4-ounce) servings.

To serve 25: Use half recipe, *except* use 1 can *each* limeade and lemonade concentrate.

Appetizer Buffet
Serves 30

Sausage Nibbles
Shrimp Tartlets
Cheesy Onion Dip   Confetti Log
Cauliflower with Anchovy
Carrot and Celery Sticks
Sesame-Cheddar Wafers
Tortilla Chips   Crackers
Red Bubble Punch

BUFFET SERVING TIP: This bountiful appetizer buffet (pictured on page 56) will serve a large number of guests in a limited amount of space. Since the menu features finger foods exclusively, even those who are standing can manage nicely. Use colorful paper plates and napkins that match your party theme, but be sure to select plates that are as sturdy as they are attractive.

Sesame-Cheddar Wafers

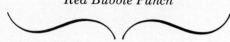

This cheesy hors d'oeuvre is good served as an accompaniment to fruit salads, too—

    1 cup shredded sharp Cheddar
        cheese (4 ounces)
    6 tablespoons butter or margarine,
        softened
    1 cup all-purpose flour
    ¼ cup sesame seed, toasted
    ½ teaspoon paprika
    ¼ teaspoon onion salt

In mixing bowl cream together shredded Cheddar cheese and butter or margarine. Thoroughly stir together flour, toasted sesame seed, paprika, and onion salt; add to butter mixture, blending thoroughly. Cover dough; chill for 1 to 2 hours.

Shape chilled dough into 36 balls. Place balls 2 inches apart on ungreased baking sheet. Flatten each ball with bottom of glass dipped in flour. Bake at 350° for 7 to 8 minutes. Makes 36 wafers.

Shrimp Tartlets

    2 cups all-purpose flour
    1 teaspoon salt
    ⅔ cup shortening
    5 to 7 tablespoons cold water
    1 3-ounce package cream cheese,
        softened
    ¼ cup dairy sour cream
    2 tablespoons cocktail sauce
    1½ teaspoons snipped fresh dillweed *or*
        ½ teaspoon dried dillweed
    2 4½-ounce cans shrimp, drained and
        coarsely chopped
    ⅓ cup finely chopped celery

Stir together flour and salt; cut in shortening till pieces are size of small peas. Sprinkle *1 tablespoon* cold water over part of mixture. Gently toss with fork; push to side of bowl. Repeat till all is moistened. Form dough into a ball. Roll to about ⅛-inch thickness; cut into 2x2-inch squares. Place in 1¾-inch miniature muffin pans, pressing to fit. Prick with fork. Bake at 400° till golden brown, about 8 minutes. Cool.

Meanwhile, blend together softened cream cheese, sour cream, cocktail sauce, dillweed, and ¼ teaspoon salt; stir in shrimp and celery. Chill thoroughly.

Before serving, spoon *1 generous teaspoon* shrimp mixture into each tart shell. Garnish with snipped parsley, if desired. (Shells may be baked ahead.) Makes 48.

Red Bubble Punch

    3 32-ounce bottles cranberry juice
        cocktail
    3 6-ounce cans frozen lemonade
        concentrate, thawed
    1 cup brandy
    3 ⅘-quart bottles pink champagne,
        chilled

Combine cranberry juice cocktail, lemonade concentrate, and brandy; chill thoroughly. Just before serving, pour juice mixture into punch bowl; carefully add champagne, pouring down side of punch bowl. Mix gently. Makes 48 (4-ounce) servings.

Sausage Nibbles

>   1 8-ounce package brown-and-serve
>   sausage links
>   1 13¼-ounce can pineapple chunks
>   ⅓ cup soy sauce
>   ¼ cup packed brown sugar
>   1 tablespoon cooking oil
>   1 clove garlic, minced
>   1 5-ounce can water chestnuts, drained
>   and halved
>   2 medium green peppers, cut in ¾-inch
>   squares

Cut sausages in thirds crosswise. Drain pineapple, reserving ½ cup syrup. Combine reserved syrup, soy, brown sugar, oil, and garlic; stir till sugar dissolves. Add sausage and water chestnuts; let stand 2 hours at room temperature or 6 hours in refrigerator. Drain. Thread *1 piece each* sausage, pineapple, water chestnut, and green pepper on short skewers. Broil 3 minutes on each side. Makes 30 appetizers.

Cauliflower with Anchovy

>   3 cups small cauliflowerets
>   ⅔ cup white wine vinegar
>   ⅔ cup salad oil
>   ¼ cup water
>   3 tablespoons sugar
>   1 medium clove garlic, minced
>   Dash bottled hot pepper sauce
>   1 small onion, sliced and separated
>   into rings
>   1 2-ounce can anchovy fillets, drained
>   and coarsely chopped
>   2 tablespoons finely chopped canned
>   pimiento

Cook cauliflowerets in small amount of boiling salted water just till crisp-tender, about 5 minutes; drain. In screw-top jar combine vinegar, oil, water, sugar, garlic, and hot pepper sauce. Cover; shake vigorously. Combine cauliflowerets, onion, anchovy, and pimiento in shallow dish; pour marinade over. Cover. Chill 8 hours or overnight; stir occasionally. Drain; serve with cocktail picks. Makes 3½ cups.

Cheesy Onion Dip

Serve this in a fondue pot—

>   1 9-ounce package frozen onions
>   in cream sauce
>   2 6-ounce rolls garlic cheese food
>   1 cup dairy sour cream
>   ¼ cup thinly sliced green onion
>   (optional)
>   ¼ teaspoon bottled hot pepper sauce
>   Tortilla chips

Prepare frozen onions in cream sauce according to package directions. Pour onion mixture into blender container; cover and chop coarsely. Return chopped onion mixture to saucepan. Cut garlic cheese food into chunks; add to onion mixture in saucepan. Heat slowly, stirring constantly, till well blended. Stir in sour cream; *3 tablespoons* of sliced green onion, if desired; and hot pepper sauce. Heat through *but do not boil.*

To serve, transfer dip to fondue pot; keep warm over fondue burner. Top with remaining green onion, if desired. Serve with tortilla chips. Makes 4 cups.

Confetti Log

>   2 8-ounce packages cream cheese,
>   softened
>   1 4-ounce container whipped cream
>   cheese with blue cheese
>   2 tablespoons milk
>   ½ cup finely chopped green pepper
>   ½ cup finely chopped radish
>   ½ cup finely chopped celery
>   ½ cup finely chopped pitted ripe olives
>   ½ cup snipped parsley
>   Assorted crackers

Blend together softened cream cheese, whipped cream cheese with blue cheese, and milk; stir in finely chopped green pepper, radish, celery, and pitted ripe olives. Mix thoroughly; chill several hours.

Shape cheese mixture into a 10x2-inch log; roll log in snipped parsley. Chill till serving time. Serve with crackers. Serves 32.

To divide: Use half recipe. Shape chilled cheese mixture into a ball, if desired.

Picnic Buffets that Travel

Make-Ahead Picnic

Serves 12 (halve for 6)

Picnic Meat Loaves
French-Fry Salad
Tomato-Cucumber Marinade
Sourdough Bread
Brownie Macaroon Cupcakes
or
Molasses-Peanut Cookies
Soft Drinks

BUFFET SERVING TIP: Although many people prefer to set up a portable buffet on a picnic table, a large, flat rock or an open, grassy area will work equally well. Be sure to pack up any leftover food and take all debris with you when you leave the area.

Tomato-Cucumber Marinade

    4 medium tomatoes, sliced
    Salt
    2 medium cucumbers, scored and thinly
       sliced (about 4 cups)
    ½ cup sliced green onion with tops
    1 cup salad oil
    ⅓ cup dry white wine
    ⅓ cup white wine vinegar
    1 tablespoon dried salad herbs, crushed
    2 teaspoons salt
    ¼ teaspoon pepper

Lightly sprinkle tomatoes with a little salt. Alternate layers of tomato, cucumber, and onion in 2 deep bowls. In screw-top jar combine oil, wine, vinegar, salad herbs, the 2 teaspoons salt, and pepper; cover and shake vigorously. Pour over vegetables. Cover and chill 5 to 6 hours to thoroughly blend flavors. Makes 12 servings.

Picnic Meat Loaves

A delightful picnic main dish—

    2 slightly beaten eggs
    2 5⅓-ounce cans evaporated milk
    1 cup cocktail sauce
    2 cups soft bread crumbs
       (3 slices bread)
    ½ cup chopped onion
    ½ cup chopped celery
    ½ cup chopped dill pickle
    2 tablespoons prepared horseradish
    2 teaspoons salt
    4 pounds ground beef

Combine first 9 ingredients. Add beef; mix well. Pat into four 7½x3½x2-inch loaf pans. Bake at 350° till done, 50 to 60 minutes. Drain; chill thoroughly. Slice at the picnic site; serve with additional cocktail sauce, if desired. Makes 12 to 16 servings.

French-Fry Salad

    2 16-ounce packages frozen French-
       fried potatoes
    ½ cup Russian salad dressing
       • • •
    2 cups sliced celery
    1 cup sliced radishes
    1 8-ounce carton sour cream dip
       with French onion
    ½ cup mayonnaise or salad dressing
    ¼ cup milk
    2 tablespoons snipped parsley
    2 tablespoons lemon juice
    1 teaspoon salt

Cut up large potatoes. In 12-inch skillet combine potatoes and Russian dressing. Cook over low heat till potatoes are defrosted. Cover and heat 2 to 4 minutes, stirring gently once or twice. Pour into mixing bowl. Combine remaining ingredients; stir into potatoes. Cover; chill well in 2 containers till picnic time. Makes 12 servings.

Picnic Meat Loaves and *French-Fry Salad* are easy to tote and easy to serve. Make-ahead foods such as these are ideal for picnics because you can thoroughly chill them before packing for the picnic.

Brownie Macaroon Cupcakes

A quick to fix picnic dessert that's sure to please young and old alike —

1 package chocolate macaroon ring cake mix

Prepare chocolate cake batter mix and coconut filling mix according to package directions. Place 36 paper bake cups in muffin pans, fill bake cups ⅔ full with chocolate cake batter. Place *1 teaspoon* coconut filling in the center of each cupcake; press filling down into chocolate cake batter. Bake at 350° till cupcakes test done, about 20 minutes. Cool on rack.

When cupcakes are cool, prepare vanilla glaze mix from package according to directions on envelope. Frost cupcakes with vanilla glaze. Makes 36 cupcakes.

Molasses-Peanut Cookies

½ cup shortening
½ cup sugar
½ cup light molasses
½ cup chunk-style peanut butter
1 egg
2 cups all-purpose flour
¼ teaspoon baking soda
¼ teaspoon baking powder
¼ teaspoon salt

In mixing bowl cream shortening and sugar; beat in molasses, peanut butter, and egg. Thoroughly stir together flour, soda, baking powder, and salt. Add to creamed mixture; mix well. Drop by rounded teaspoonfuls 2 inches apart onto ungreased cookie sheet; flatten slightly with fork. Bake at 375° till done, about 8 minutes. Makes 48.

Tailgate Picnic
Serves 16 (halve for 8)

Barbecued Ham Sandwiches
Shoestring Potatoes
Baked Beans
Tossed Italian Salad
Pickled Cherries
Fresh Fruit
Lemonade   Coffee

BUFFET SERVING TIP: Taking a group of your friends to a sports event? Make the trip more enjoyable by planning a picnic buffet served from the back of a station wagon or hatchback. Assemble the sandwiches at home, wrap them in foil or clear plastic wrap, and carry them in an insulated carrier. Bring paper cups for the barbecue sauce dip.

Barbecued Ham Sandwiches

⅔ cup catsup
½ cup unsweetened pineapple juice
¼ cup packed brown sugar
3 tablespoons lemon juice
2 tablespoons prepared mustard
1 tablespoon prepared horseradish
1 teaspoon paprika
• • •
1 3-pound canned ham
16 slices Swiss cheese
2 loaves sliced rye bread, buttered
(32 slices)

In medium saucepan combine catsup, pineapple juice, sugar, lemon juice, mustard, prepared horseradish, and paprika. Cover; simmer sauce for 10 minutes. Remove from heat; chill sauce thoroughly.

Slice canned ham very thin. Assemble ham slices and Swiss cheese slices on *half* of the buttered bread slices. Top with remaining bread slices; wrap sandwiches individually. Serve with chilled barbecue sauce for dipping. Makes 16 sandwiches.

Tossed Italian Salad
Lettuce stays crisp in ice till picnic time —

10 cups torn lettuce (2 medium heads)
Ice cubes
2 10-ounce packages frozen mixed vegetables, cooked, drained, and chilled
1 15-ounce can garbanzo beans, drained
4 ounces mozzarella cheese, cut in strips
½ cup thinly sliced pepperoni
1 cup Italian salad dressing

Place lettuce in large plastic bag with a few ice cubes; tie closed. In another bag combine cooked mixed vegetables, garbanzo beans, cheese strips, and sliced pepperoni; tie closed. Pour Italian salad dressing into screw-top jar; cover.

At serving time, remove ice cubes from lettuce and pour off water. Add vegetable-meat mixture to drained lettuce in bag. Pour in dressing; shake well to coat all ingredients thoroughly. Makes 16 servings.

Pickled Cherries
You'll be glad that you home-canned this spicy relish while the cherries were in season —

1½ cups water
½ cup vinegar
¼ cup sugar
1 inch stick cinnamon, broken up
1 teaspoon mustard seed
½ teaspoon whole allspice
½ teaspoon salt
¼ teaspoon whole cloves
• • •
1 quart tart red cherries with stems

In saucepan combine water, vinegar, sugar, cinnamon, mustard seed, allspice, salt, and cloves. Bring to a boil; simmer 8 minutes.

Wash cherries; do not remove stems or pits. Pack into hot, clean jars, leaving ¾-inch headspace. Pour boiling spice liquid over cherries, leaving ½-inch headspace. Adjust lids. Process 5 minutes in boiling water bath. Let stand at least 1 week. Drain before serving. Makes 2 pints.

Roadside Picnic

Serves 8

Deviled Chicken
Potato Chips
Carrot-Bean Relish
Cherry Tomatoes   Ripe Olives
German Oat Cake
or
Spice Cake
Cold Beer   Soft Drinks

BUFFET SERVING TIP: Make picnic plans for this menu that include a means of keeping the cold chicken, crisp relishes, and chilled beverages cold until they are eaten. Insulated containers and large ice chests are useful especially when you pack blocks of ice with the food to keep the temperature down. Remember that these picnic foods not only taste better but are safer to eat if they are handled properly.

Deviled Chicken

Curry accents the crispy chicken coating—

  1 cup fine dry bread crumbs
  4 teaspoons onion powder
  4 teaspoons curry powder
1½ teaspoons salt
  1 teaspoon dry mustard
  ½ teaspoon garlic powder
  ½ teaspoon paprika
    Dash cayenne
  2 2½-pound ready-to-cook broiler-fryer
    chickens, cut up
    Milk

Combine fine dry bread crumbs, onion powder, curry, salt, dry mustard, garlic powder, paprika, and cayenne; mix well. Dip chicken pieces in the milk, then in the crumb mixture. Place chicken, skin side up, in greased, shallow baking pan. Bake at 375° till done, about 1 hour. Chill chicken thoroughly. Makes 8 servings.

Carrot-Bean Relish

A colorful, crunchy side dish—

Combine one 8¼-ounce can sliced carrots, drained; one 8-ounce can cut green beans, drained; ¼ cup chopped green pepper; and ¼ cup chopped onion. Combine ⅓ cup vinegar; ¼ cup sugar; 3 tablespoons salad oil; 2 tablespoons snipped parsley; ½ teaspoon dried oregano, crushed; and ¼ teaspoon salt. Stir till sugar dissolves. Pour over vegetables; toss gently. Cover and chill overnight.

Before serving, toss relish again to coat vegetables; drain. Makes 2½ cups.

German Oat Cake

1¼ cups boiling water
  1 cup quick-cooking rolled oats
  ½ cup butter or margarine
  1 4-ounce package sweet cooking
    chocolate, broken up
1½ cups all-purpose flour
  1 cup granulated sugar
  1 teaspoon baking soda
  ½ teaspoon salt
  1 cup packed brown sugar
  3 eggs
    Caramel Nut Topping

In medium mixing bowl pour boiling water over quick-cooking rolled oats; add butter or margarine and chocolate. Let stand 20 minutes; stir till well combined.

In large mixing bowl thoroughly stir together flour, granulated sugar, soda, and salt. Stir in brown sugar. Add eggs and oatmeal mixture. Beat at low speed of electric mixer till thoroughly combined. Scrape sides of bowl. Turn into greased and floured 13x9x2-inch baking pan. Bake at 350° till cake tests done, 35 to 40 minutes.

Spread Caramel Nut Topping over hot cake. Broil 4 to 5 inches from heat till bubbly, about 1 minute. Serve warm or cool.

Caramel Nut Topping: In small saucepan cook and stir ¾ cup packed brown sugar, 6 tablespoons butter or margarine, and ¼ cup light cream till mixture comes to boiling; reduce heat. Simmer till thick, 2 to 3 minutes; stirring often. Add ½ cup chopped pecans.

Buffet-Style Barbecues

Backyard Barbecue

Serves 6 (double for 12)

*Orange-Ginger Ham Grill
Italian Macaroni Salad
Corn-Asparagus Relish
Breadsticks
or
Barbecued Pumpernickel
Melon Ambrosia
Cold Beer*

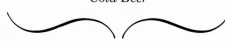

BUFFET SERVING TIP: Move cooked foods to the edge of the grill to keep them warm without overcooking. To serve cold foods, wheel a serving cart or other small table near the grill. Let friends fill their plates, then eat at the patio table.

Orange-Ginger Ham Grill

¼ cup frozen orange juice concentrate, thawed
¼ cup dry white wine
1 teaspoon dry mustard
¼ teaspoon ground ginger
1 1½- to 2-pound fully cooked ham slice, cut 1 inch thick
6 canned pineapple slices

Combine orange juice concentrate, wine, mustard, and ginger. Brush sauce over ham. Grill over *medium* coals for 10 to 15 minutes, brushing with sauce occasionally. Turn ham and grill second side 10 to 15 minutes more, brushing with sauce.

Grill pineapple slices alongside the ham, brushing frequently with sauce. Place pineapple atop ham during last 5 to 10 minutes of grilling. Garnish with orange slices, if desired. Makes 6 servings.

Italian Macaroni Salad

Serve this tasty macaroni mixture at your next cookout instead of traditional potato salad—

1¼ cups tiny shell macaroni (4 ounces)
¼ cup Italian salad dressing
1 8-ounce carton cream-style cottage cheese (1 cup)
1 cup dairy sour cream
½ cup chopped celery
¼ cup chopped green pepper
1 hard-cooked egg, chopped
2 tablespoons milk
1 tablespoon sliced green onion with tops
½ teaspoon salt

Cook macaroni according to package directions; drain well. While macaroni is still hot, toss it with Italian dressing; let stand 30 minutes. Stir in cottage cheese, sour cream, celery, green pepper, egg, milk, onion, and salt. Chill. Makes 6 servings.

Corn-Asparagus Relish

Colorful vegetables chill in a tangy marinade—

1 10-ounce package frozen whole kernel corn, cooked and drained
1 9-ounce package frozen cut asparagus, cooked and drained
1 envelope garlic salad dressing mix (enough for 1 cup dressing)
½ cup tarragon vinegar
⅓ cup salad oil
2 tablespoons water
2 tablespoons chopped canned pimiento
1 tablespoon sugar

Combine drained corn and asparagus. In a screw-top jar combine salad dressing mix, tarragon vinegar, oil, water, pimiento, and sugar; cover and shake vigorously. Pour dressing over vegetables. Cover; refrigerate 8 hours or overnight, stirring occasionally. Drain before serving. Makes about 3 cups.

Combine the informality of a barbecue with buffet service for a relaxing, congenial evening with friends. To highlight the evening, serve *Orange-Ginger Ham Grill* with glazed pineapple slices.

Barbecued Pumpernickel

A jiffy bread fix-up that heats on the grill —

> **1 1-pound round loaf unsliced pumper-
> nickel bread**
> **½ cup butter or margarine, softened**
> **¼ cup grated Parmesan cheese**
> **3 tablespoons special blend seasoning
> sauce**
> **2 tablespoons snipped parsley**

Cut bread in ½-inch-thick slices, cutting to but not through bottom crust. Combine butter, Parmesan, seasoning sauce, and parsley. Spread mixture between every other slice of bread. Make 1 *lengthwise* slice down center of bread, cutting to but not through bottom crust. Wrap loaf in foil. Heat foil-wrapped bread over *slow* coals till warm through, 25 to 30 minutes. Makes 1 loaf.

Melon Ambrosia

> **2 cups honeydew melon balls**
> **2 cups cantaloupe balls**
> **2 cups watermelon cubes**
> • • •
> **⅔ cup sugar**
> **⅓ cup water**
> **3 tablespoons lemon juice**
> **3 tablespoons lime juice**
> **⅓ cup flaked coconut**

In a large bowl combine honeydew melon balls, cantaloupe balls, and watermelon cubes. Combine sugar, water, lemon juice, and lime juice; stir till sugar dissolves. Pour juice mixture over fruit in bowl; toss lightly. Cover; chill 4 to 6 hours, stirring occasionally. Before serving, sprinkle coconut over the top. Makes 6 servings.

Frank or Burger Barbecue
Serves 6

Best Hamdogs or *Reverse Burgers*
Potato Chips
Harvest Cream
or
Tossed Salad   Vinegar and Oil
Dill Pickles   Ripe Olives
Blueberry Pie
Frosty Lime Fizz

BUFFET SERVING TIP: The informality of an outdoor barbecue suggests the use of paper or plastic serving dishes. Since the weather may not always cooperate, it is a good idea to make advance arrangements for moving the buffet indoors on relatively short notice.

Best Hamdogs

1 cup finely chopped fully cooked ham
   or luncheon meat
3 tablespoons sweet pickle relish
2 tablespoons finely chopped onion
2 tablespoons prepared mustard
2 tablespoons mayonnaise or salad
   dressing
   • • •
1 pound frankfurters (8 to 10)
8 to 10 slices bacon
   Bottled barbecue sauce
8 to 10 frankfurter buns, split and
   toasted

In bowl combine chopped ham or luncheon meat, sweet pickle relish, finely chopped onion, prepared mustard, and mayonnaise or salad dressing. Slit frankfurters, *cutting almost to ends and only ¾ of the way through.* Stuff franks with ham mixture; wrap with bacon and secure with wooden picks.

Grill frankfurters over *hot* coals till filling is hot and bacon is crisp; brush occasionally with barbecue sauce. Serve in toasted buns. Makes 8 to 10 servings.

Reverse Burgers

1½ pounds ground beef
½ cup chili sauce
⅓ cup chopped green onion
1 teaspoon salt
6 slices French bread, cut 1 inch thick
   Butter or margarine, softened

Combine first 4 ingredients; mix well. Spread *both* sides of bread first with butter, then with meat mixture, using about ⅓ cup meat per side. Grill over *medium* coals 5 to 6 minutes; turn and grill till meat is done, 5 to 6 minutes longer. Makes 6 servings.

Harvest Cream

2 cups apple juice
1 3-ounce package lemon-flavored
   gelatin
1 cup chopped unpeeled apple
¼ cup chopped pecans
1 2-ounce package dessert topping mix

In a saucepan heat *1 cup* of the juice to boiling; add gelatin. Stir to dissolve. Add remaining juice. Chill till partially set. Add apple and pecans to *1 cup* of the gelatin. Pour into 5½-cup mold; chill till almost firm. Prepare topping mix according to package directions; fold into remaining gelatin. Pour over first layer. Chill till firm. Serves 6.

Frosty Lime Fizz

1 12-ounce can unsweetened pineapple
   juice, chilled (1½ cups)
½ cup sugar
½ cup lime juice
1 quart lime sherbet
1 28-ounce bottle lemon-lime carbonated
   beverage, chilled

Put first 3 ingredients in blender container; spoon in *half* of the sherbet. Adjust lid; blend smooth. Pour ½ cup mixture into *each* of six 12-ounce glasses. Add a scoop of sherbet to each glass. Fill glasses with carbonated beverage. Makes 6 servings.

Fisherman's Luck Barbecue

Serves 12

Barbecued Bass Steaks
Classy Carrots
Potato Salad
Crisp Relishes   Sliced Tomatoes
Chive Bread
Fresh Fruit Bars
Iced Tea   Beer

BUFFET SERVING TIP: What better way to swap fish stories with fishing buddies than to invite them to your backyard for a fish barbecue. Don't hesitate to ask the luckiest fisherman present to grill the fish while you keep a watchful eye on the vegetables and bread.

Fresh Fruit Bars

1 roll refrigerated sugar cookie dough

• • •

1 8-ounce package cream cheese, softened
⅓ cup sugar
½ teaspoon vanilla
2 cups sliced fresh peaches
2 cups fresh raspberries
¼ cup apricot preserves *or* orange marmalade
1 tablespoon water

Cut refrigerated sugar cookie dough into ⅛-inch-thick slices. Arrange cookie dough in bottom of an ungreased 15½x10½x1-inch baking pan *or* a 14-inch pizza pan, overlapping edges of dough slightly. Press to even dough. Bake at 375° for 12 minutes; cool.

In mixing bowl combine the cream cheese, sugar, and vanilla; beat till smooth. Spread the cheese mixture onto the cooled cookie crust; arrange sliced peaches and raspberries on top. Combine apricot preserves or orange marmalade and water; spoon evenly over fruits. Chill thoroughly. Cut into 3x2-inch bars or diamonds. Makes 25 cookies.

Barbecued Bass Steaks

4 pounds fresh or frozen bass steaks
⅔ cup cooking oil
2 tablespoons sesame seed, toasted
2 tablespoons lemon juice
2 tablespoons wine vinegar
2 tablespoons soy sauce
1 teaspoon salt

Thaw frozen fish. Cut into 12 portions. Place fish in single layer in two shallow dishes. Combine cooking oil, toasted sesame seed, lemon juice, wine vinegar, soy sauce, and salt. Pour mixture over fish. Marinate for 30 minutes at room temperature; turn fish once. Remove fish; reserve marinade.

Place marinated fish in well-greased wire broiler basket. Grill over *medium-hot* coals for 10 minutes. Turn fish and baste with reserved marinade. Grill till fish flakes easily when tested with a fork, 5 to 8 minutes longer. Makes 12 servings.

Classy Carrots

3 16-ounce cans sliced carrots
½ cup orange marmalade
3 tablespoons butter or margarine
3 tablespoons orange liqueur

In large, heavy skillet heat carrots through; drain. Add marmalade, butter, and liqueur; simmer over *slow* coals, stirring gently, till butter melts and carrots are coated. Season with salt and pepper. Serves 12.

Chive Bread

2 unsliced loaves French bread
1 cup butter or margarine, softened
⅔ cup grated Parmesan cheese
½ cup finely snipped chives

Slash loaves in 1-inch slices, *cutting to, but not through* bottom crust. Blend together butter, Parmesan, and chives; spread mixture on one side of each bread slice. Wrap loaves individually in foil. Heat on edge of grill 20 to 30 minutes; turn often.

Company Cookout

Serves 6

Beef and Cheese Pinwheels
Barbecued Chicken
Grilled Corn on the Cob
Vegetable Salad Rolls
Banana Brickle Bars
Iced Tea

BUFFET SERVING TIP: Savoring the aroma of foods on the grill is one of the thrills of outdoor cooking. Another is watching the master chef at work. Let guests enjoy both by serving the appetizers in the backyard.

Grilled Corn on the Cob

Husk and remove silk from 6 ears of corn. Place each ear on a sheet of heavy foil. Combine ½ cup butter or margarine, softened; 1 teaspoon dried rosemary, crushed; and ½ teaspoon dried marjoram, crushed. Spread about *1 tablespoon* mixture over each ear of corn. Wrap securely, using drugstore wrap. Place on coals till done, 12 to 15 minutes; turn often. Serves 6.

To make *Vegetable Salad Rolls,* use a fork to scoop out rolls before filling with salad. Reserve centers of rolls for use in stuffings.

Barbecued Chicken

1 8-ounce can tomato sauce
½ cup olive oil
½ cup orange juice
¼ cup vinegar
1½ teaspoons dried oregano, crushed
1 teaspoon salt
6 peppercorns
1 clove garlic, minced

• • •

2 whole chicken breasts, halved lengthwise
4 chicken legs including thighs
¼ cup honey
½ teaspoon dry mustard

In large screw-top jar combine tomato sauce, oil, orange juice, vinegar, oregano, salt, peppercorns, and garlic; cover and shake well. In shallow dish pour mixture over chicken. Cover and marinate 2 hours at room temperature or overnight in refrigerator; turn chicken pieces occasionally.

Drain; reserve marinade. Grill chicken over *medium* coals for 45 to 50 minutes. Brush with marinade; turn frequently. Just before serving, brush chicken with mixture of honey and mustard. Serves 6.

Vegetable Salad Rolls

½ cup chopped green pepper
½ cup chopped seeded cucumber
½ cup chopped seeded tomato
½ cup chopped celery
2 tablespoons chopped red onion
2 tablespoons snipped parsley
2 tablespoons chopped dill pickle
⅓ cup sour cream dip with garlic
¼ cup mayonnaise or salad dressing
¼ teaspoon salt
6 hard rolls

Combine chopped green pepper, cucumber, tomato, celery, onion, parsley, and dill pickle. Combine sour cream dip, mayonnaise, and salt; gently fold into vegetables. Split rolls; scoop out centers, Fill rolls with salad mixture. Wrap and chill till serving time. Makes 6 servings.

Beef and Cheese Pinwheels

1 4-ounce package sliced smoked beef
1 5-ounce jar sharp process American
   cheese spread
¼ cup snipped parsley
2 tablespoons crumbled blue cheese
2 tablespoons dry white wine

Lay pieces of smoked beef out flat and pat together with edges overlapping slightly to make three 8x6-inch rectangles. Mix sharp process American cheese spread, parsley, and blue cheese; beat in wine. Spread ⅓ *cup* cheese mixture evenly over each beef rectangle. Roll up rectangles, jelly-roll style, beginning at long side. Wrap in waxed paper; chill thoroughly.

At serving time, cut each roll in ½-inch slices with very sharp knife. Serve on cocktail picks. Makes about 48.

Banana Brickle Bars

1 package 2-layer-size banana cake mix
½ cup butter or margarine, melted
1 slightly beaten egg
1 package butter brickle frosting mix
   (for 2-layer cake)
1 8-ounce package cream cheese,
   softened
2 eggs
½ cup chopped walnuts, toasted

Combine first 3 ingredients; pat in bottom of 13x9x2-inch baking pan. Combine frosting mix and cheese; beat at low speed of electric mixer for 2 minutes. Reserve 1 cup frosting and cover. Add 2 eggs to remaining frosting. Beat well. Pour over mixture in baking pan. Bake at 350° for 25 to 30 minutes. Cool. Frost with reserved frosting. Sprinkle with nuts. Cut into bars. Makes 30.

Outdoor chefs who concentrate their culinary talents on chicken will delight in trying this version of *Barbecued Chicken*. Marinated in sauce, the tender bird is brushed with a honey glaze before serving.

Sideboard Specials After the Game

He-Man Buffet
Serves 8

Beef-Stuffed Pork Roast
Baked Rice   Buttered Corn
Tossed Greens   Caesar Dressing
Dill Carrot Sticks
Rye Rolls   Butter
Harvey Wallbanger Cake
Coffee

BUFFET SERVING TIP: Make a festive occasion out of the next big TV sportscast by inviting fellow fans to watch the game at your house. Then, treat them to a feast afterward.

Harvey Wallbanger Cake

    1 package 2-layer-size orange cake mix
    1 3⅝- or 3¾-ounce package *instant*
       vanilla pudding mix
    4 eggs
    ½ cup cooking oil
    ½ cup orange juice
    ½ cup Galliano
    2 tablespoons vodka
       Glaze

In large mixing bowl combine cake and pudding mixes. Add eggs, oil, orange juice, Galliano, and vodka. Beat at low speed of electric mixer ½ minute; beat at medium speed 5 minutes. (Do not underbeat.) Scrape bowl often. Pour into greased and floured 10-inch fluted tube pan; bake at 350° for 45 minutes. Cool in pan 10 minutes; remove cake to rack. Pour Glaze over warm cake.

Glaze: In a small bowl combine 1 cup sifted powdered sugar, 1 tablespoon orange juice, 1 tablespoon Galliano, and 1 teaspoon vodka. Mix until smooth.

Beef-Stuffed Pork Roast

    1 14-ounce bottle catsup
    ½ cup chili sauce
    ⅓ cup wine vinegar
    ¼ cup packed brown sugar
    2 tablespoons prepared mustard
    2 tablespoons lemon juice
    2 tablespoons Worcestershire sauce
    2 tablespoons cooking oil
    2 tablespoons bottled steak sauce
    1 teaspoon dry mustard
    ¼ teaspoon salt
    ¼ teaspoon pepper
    1 clove garlic, minced
              • • •
    1 3-pound boneless pork loin roast
    ½ pound ground beef
    ¼ cup chopped onion
    1 small clove garlic, minced
    ¼ teaspoon salt
       Dash pepper
    1 6-ounce can sliced mushrooms, drained
    ¼ cup fine dry bread crumbs
    ¼ cup grated Parmesan cheese

In medium saucepan combine first 13 ingredients; simmer 30 minutes. Remove barbecue sauce from heat; set aside.

To butterfly pork loin, split meat lengthwise almost all the way to opposite side, then spread open flat. Pound out to 15x10-inch rectangle, about ¾ inch thick. Brush top with ¼ *cup* of the barbecue sauce.

Combine ground beef, onion, garlic, the remaining ¼ teaspoon salt, dash pepper, and ¼ *cup* of the barbecue sauce; spread mixture evenly over roast. Press mushrooms into ground beef. Sprinkle bread crumbs and Parmesan over meat and mushrooms. Roll up jelly-roll fashion, beginning with narrow side; tie several places with string. Place the meat on a rack in shallow roasting pan. Roast, uncovered, at 325° about 2½ hours. Baste with barbecue sauce during last 20 minutes. Serve with remaining sauce. Garnish with celery leaves, if desired. Serves 8.

If your favorite armchair quarterback occasionally enjoys calling the plays in the kitchen, let him prepare *Beef-Stuffed Pork Roast* before the game. All the coaching he needs is given in the recipe.

Baked Rice

⅓ cup finely chopped celery
⅓ cup finely chopped green pepper
¼ cup butter or margarine
1½ cups uncooked long grain rice
½ envelope onion soup mix (¼ cup)
1 teaspoon instant beef bouillon
   granules
½ teaspoon salt
3½ cups water

Cook celery and green pepper in butter till tender. Add rice; cook and stir till lightly browned. Remove from heat; stir in soup mix, bouillon granules, and salt. Pour into 1½-quart casserole; let stand till 1 hour before meal. Stir in water. Cover; bake at 325° for 30 minutes. Fluff with fork. Cover; bake till tender, about 30 minutes more. Serves 8.

Dill Carrot Sticks

6 medium carrots (about 1 pound)
1 cup vinegar
1 cup water
¾ cup sugar
1 tablespoon mustard seed
1 head fresh dillweed *or* ½ teaspoon
   dried dillweed

Peel carrots and cut in 3-inch lengths. Cook in boiling water 10 minutes. Drain carrots; cut lengthwise into quarters.

In saucepan combine vinegar, water, sugar, mustard seed, and fresh or dried dillweed. Simmer mixture for 10 minutes. Add carrot sticks; simmer 1 minute longer. Cool carrot sticks in the liquid. Cover and refrigerate 8 hours or overnight. Drain carrots thoroughly before serving. Makes 3 cups.

Spectator's Spread
Serves 12

Tomato Soup
Surf Boards
Tangy Cauliflower Salad
Ice Cream Roll
Milk　　Coffee

BUFFET SERVING TIP: As a first course, offer steaming-hot soup from a sideboard away from the main buffet. Let friends ladle soup into mugs, then select from a choice of garnishes such as popcorn, shredded cheese, crumbled bacon, or croutons. Have spoons available for those who prefer not to sip.

Tangy Cauliflower Salad

    2 medium heads cauliflower, separated
        into cauliflowerets (about 8 cups)
    4 medium carrots, cut in 2-inch
        julienne strips (2 cups)
      Salt
      Pepper
            • • •
    ⅔ cup French salad dressing
    1 tablespoon lemon juice
    ¼ teaspoon dried basil, crushed
    ½ cup crumbled blue cheese (2 ounces)
      Lettuce
    2 small avocados, peeled, pitted, and
        sliced

Cut cauliflowerets in half lengthwise. In large saucepan cook cauliflower and carrot strips in boiling salted water till tender, 8 to 10 minutes. Drain thoroughly. Season vegetables with salt and pepper.

Combine French dressing, lemon juice, and basil; toss dressing mixture with vegetables and blue cheese. Cover and refrigerate at least 4 hours, stirring once or twice.

At serving time, toss vegetables lightly and spoon into lettuce-lined bowl. Garnish with avocado slices. Makes 12 servings.

Surf Boards

    12 individual French rolls
    ¼ cup butter or margarine, softened
    2 7½-ounce cans crab meat, drained,
        flaked, and cartilage removed
    2 4½-ounce cans shrimp, drained
    2 cups finely chopped celery
    1½ cups mayonnaise or salad dressing
    ½ cup sweet pickle relish
    ¼ cup finely chopped onion
    2 tablespoons lemon juice
    1 teaspoon Worcestershire sauce

Split rolls lengthwise; spread with butter. Mix remaining ingredients, 1 teaspoon salt, and dash pepper. Spread on bottom halves of rolls; cover with tops. Serves 12.

Ice Cream Roll

    2 cups crumbled soft coconut macaroons
    ¼ cup dry sherry
    1 quart vanilla ice cream, softened
    1 cup dairy sour cream
    4 egg whites
    ¾ cup granulated sugar
    4 egg yolks
    ½ teaspoon vanilla
    ⅔ cup sifted cake flour
    ¼ cup unsweetened cocoa powder
    1 teaspoon baking powder
      Sifted powdered sugar

Combine crumbs and sherry. Stir in ice cream. Add sour cream; mix well. Freeze. Beat egg whites to soft peaks; add ½ *cup* of the granulated sugar; beat to stiff peaks. Beat egg yolks till thick and lemon-colored; beat in remaining granulated sugar. Add vanilla. Fold into whites. Thoroughly stir together flour, cocoa powder, baking powder, and ¼ teaspoon salt; fold into egg mixture. Spread in greased and lightly floured 15½x 10½x1-inch baking pan. Bake at 375° for 10 to 12 minutes. Immediately turn out on towel sprinkled with powdered sugar. Starting at narrow end, roll cake and towel together. Cool on rack. Stir ice cream to soften. Unroll cake; spread with ice cream. Roll up; wrap in foil. Freeze. Slice. Serves 12.

Snow Country Buffet

Serves 8

Chuck Wagon Stew
Honey-Oatmeal Bread   Butter
Apple Wedges   Tangerines
Choco-Date Cake
Coffee

BUFFET SERVING TIP: This menu will travel with you to ski slopes or hockey rink if you pack hot stew and coffee in insulated jugs. If you prefer to eat at home, reheat the stew while guests remove coats and boots.

Honey-Oatmeal Bread

4½ to 4¾ cups whole wheat flour
3 packages active dry yeast
2 cups milk
⅓ cup honey
¼ cup cooking oil
1 tablespoon salt
• • •
½ cup Scotch oats

In large mixing bowl combine *2 cups* of the flour and yeast. In saucepan heat milk, honey, oil, and salt just till warm (115-120°). Add to dry mixture in mixing bowl. Beat at low speed of electric mixer for ½ minute, scraping sides of bowl constantly. Beat 3 minutes at high speed. By hand, stir in oats and enough of the remaining flour to make a stiff dough. Turn out onto lightly floured surface. Knead till smooth and elastic, 8 to 10 minutes. Shape into a ball. Place in lightly greased bowl, turning once to grease surface. Cover; let rise in warm place till double, about 45 minutes.

Punch down; turn out on lightly floured surface. Divide in half. Cover; let rest 10 minutes. Shape into two loaves; place in two greased 8½x4½x2½-inch loaf pans. Cover; let rise in warm place till double, about 30 minutes. Bake at 375° for 35 to 40 minutes. Remove from pans; cool. Makes 2.

Chuck Wagon Stew

If you don't plan to carry the stew with you, refrigerate it and heat it after you get home—

In Dutch oven slowly brown 2 pounds beef stew meat cut in 1½-inch cubes in 2 table-spoons hot shortening. Drain one 16-ounce can tomatoes, reserving juice. Set the toma-toes aside. Add enough water to reserved tomato juice to make 2 cups. Add juice to meat with 1 medium onion, sliced; 1 clove garlic, minced; 1 tablespoon salt; 1 teaspoon sugar; 1 teaspoon Worcestershire sauce; and ¼ teaspoon dried thyme, crushed. Cover; simmer 1½ hours. Stir occasionally.

Add 6 carrots, cut in 1-inch slices; ½ pound small white onions *or* one 16-ounce can boiled onions, drained; 3 potatoes, peeled and quar-tered; and ½ cup celery sliced in ½-inch pieces. Cover; simmer 20 minutes. Add re-served tomatoes. Cook till vegetables are tender, about 15 minutes. Skim off fat. Mea-sure liquid; for each 3 cups, blend ½ cup cold water and 3 tablespoons all-purpose flour. Add to stew; cook and stir till thickened and bubbly. Cook 5 minutes more. Serves 6 to 8.

Choco-Date Cake

The topping bakes on the cake—

½ pound pitted dates, coarsely chopped
1 cup boiling water
1 cup sugar
½ cup shortening
1 teaspoon vanilla
1 egg
1½ cups all-purpose flour
2 tablespoons unsweetened cocoa powder
1 teaspoon baking soda
½ cup chopped walnuts
½ cup semisweet chocolate pieces

Combine dates with water; cool to room temperature. Cream sugar and shortening till light. Add vanilla and egg; beat well. Stir together thoroughly flour, cocoa, soda, and ¼ teaspoon salt; add to creamed mixture al-ternately with date mixture, beating after each addition. Turn into greased and floured 13x9x2-inch baking pan. Sprinkle with nuts and chocolate. Bake at 350° 25 to 30 minutes.

Victory Supper

Serves 24

Blue Cheese Spread   Crackle Thins
Booya
Assorted Rolls   Butter
Relishes
Cherry-Almond Ice Cream
Beer   Coffee

BUFFET SERVING TIP: Your friends will relish the hard-fought victory even more when they return from a cold stadium to a soup buffet in the warmth of your home. To avoid last-minute panic, prepare foods and table in advance. Let guests munch on appetizers while you reheat the soup.

Cherry-Almond Ice Cream

> 1 8-ounce jar red maraschino cherries
> 2 cups sugar
> ⅓ cup all-purpose flour
> ½ teaspoon salt
> 4½ cups milk
> 5 beaten eggs
> 4 cups whipping cream
> 1 cup slivered almonds, toasted
> 4 teaspoons vanilla
> 1 teaspoon almond extract
> Few drops red food coloring

Drain cherries; reserve syrup. Add water to syrup to equal ½ cup; set aside. Finely chop cherries; set aside. In large saucepan combine sugar, flour, and salt; gradually stir in milk and reserved cherry syrup. Cook, stirring constantly, over low heat till thickened and bubbly. Stir a moderate amount of mixture into eggs; return all to saucepan. Cook and stir 1 minute more. Chill thoroughly.

Stir in chopped cherries and remaining ingredients. Pour into a 1-gallon ice cream freezer container. Freeze according to freezer manufacturer's directions. After freezing, let ripen about 4 hours. Makes 3 quarts.

Crackle Thins

Corn chips that you can make yourself—

> ½ cup milk
> 3 tablespoons cooking oil
> ¼ teaspoon Worcestershire sauce
> Dash bottled hot pepper sauce
> • • •
> 1 cup yellow cornmeal
> ½ cup all-purpose flour
> ¾ teaspoon salt
> ¼ teaspoon baking soda
> • • •
> Salt

Combine milk, cooking oil, Worcestershire sauce, and dash hot pepper sauce. In a medium mixing bowl thoroughly stir together cornmeal, flour, ¾ teaspoon salt, and baking soda. Add the milk mixture; stir till dough forms a ball. Turn dough onto a lightly floured surface. Knead gently 5 minutes.

Divide the dough in half. Place each half on a greased baking sheet. Roll each into a 12-inch square. Cut rolled dough into 1½-inch squares. Sprinkle with salt. Bake at 350° till golden brown, 12 to 15 minutes. (Edges of crackers will be browner than center.) Cool slightly before removing from baking sheet. To preserve crispness store crackers in loosely covered container. Makes about 10 dozen crackers.

To divide: Use half recipe, *except* use 1 tablespoon cooking oil, dash Worcestershire sauce, and ¼ teaspoon salt in dough. Also omit direction to divide dough in half.

Blue Cheese Spread

> 1 envelope unflavored gelatin
> 2 cups dairy sour cream
> 1 cup cream-style cottage cheese
> ¼ cup crumbled blue cheese
> 2 tablespoons Italian salad dressing

Soften gelatin in ¼ cup cold water. Cook and stir over low heat till gelatin dissolves. Stir into sour cream. Add remaining ingredients; beat with electric mixer till smooth. Pour into 4-cup ring mold. Cover; chill till firm. Unmold to serve. Makes 3½ cups.

Booya

3 pounds beef short ribs
2 pounds cubed beef
2 pounds cubed pork
2½ pounds soup bones, split
1½ pounds beef oxtails
4 large onions, sliced
6 cups parsley sprigs
½ cup dry split peas
½ cup dry lima beans
¼ cup salt
1½ to 2 tablespoons pepper
1 tablespoon dried oregano, crushed
1 tablespoon dried basil, crushed
1 tablespoon paprika
1 teaspoon garlic salt
1 teaspoon dried savory, crushed

• • •

1 large head red cabbage, chopped
   (15 cups)

3 cups diced carrot (about 1 pound)
3 cups diced rutabaga
3 cups diced celery (about 1 pound)
1 cup diced green pepper
2 28-ounce cans tomatoes
2 15½-ounce cans cut green beans
1 17-ounce can peas
1 17-ounce can whole kernel corn

In very large kettle combine meats, bones, onions, parsley, split peas, lima beans, salt, pepper, oregano, basil, paprika, garlic salt, and savory; add water to cover. Bring to a boil; reduce heat. Cover; simmer till meat is very tender, 5 hours.

Remove meat from bones and cube; discard bones. Skim fat from stock. Return meat to kettle; add cabbage, carrot, rutabaga, celery, and green pepper. Cover; simmer 1 hour more. Add *undrained* canned vegetables. Simmer 30 minutes. Makes 3½ gallons.

Booya, a hearty Bohemian stew, is a slow-simmering mixture of meats, vegetables, and seasonings that can't be rushed. It's a satisfying meal-in-a-bowl that is well worth every minute it takes to create.

Holiday Meals from the Buffet

Easter Dinner
Serves 12

Cranberry-Glazed Ham
Parslied Sweet Potatoes
Buttered Broccoli Spears
Lemon-Fruit Salad
Pickled Eggs
Crescent Rolls   Butter
Mocha Dessert
Milk   Coffee

BUFFET SERVING TIP: Before dinner, arrange flatware, napkins, and water on card tables or one large table. And if the buffet table is congested, set the beverage on a small table or tea cart near the end of the line.

Lemon-Fruit Salad

- 1 11-ounce can mandarin orange sections
- 1 8¾-ounce can peach slices
- 1 8¾-ounce can pineapple tidbits
- 1 8¼-ounce can light seedless grapes
- ¼ cup sliced maraschino cherries
- 1 3¼-ounce package lemon tapioca pudding mix
- 2 tablespoons lemon juice
- 1 cup tiny marshmallows
- 2 cups frozen whipped dessert topping, thawed

Drain fruits; reserve 1½ cups syrup. Prepare pudding according to package directions, *except* substitute reserved 1½ cups syrup for milk called for on package. Stir in lemon juice. Cover surface of pudding with waxed paper; cool. Remove paper. Dice peaches; fold into pudding with other fruits and marshmallows. Fold in thawed topping. Chill well. Makes 12 servings.

Pickled Eggs

In saucepan combine 1 cup tarragon vinegar; 1 cup water; 2 tablespoons sugar; 1 teaspoon salt; ½ teaspoon celery seed; 1 clove garlic, minced; and 2 bay leaves. Bring to a boil; simmer 30 minutes. Cool. Shell 12 hard-cooked eggs; pour vinegar mixture over eggs in crock, jar, or deep bowl. Cover; refrigerate 2 to 3 days. Makes 12.

Mocha Dessert

- 1 cup finely crushed graham crackers (14 crackers)
- 1 tablespoon sugar
- ¼ cup butter or margarine, melted
- ¾ cup sugar
- ¼ cup unsweetened cocoa powder
- 2 envelopes unflavored gelatin
- 2 teaspoons instant coffee crystals
- ¼ teaspoon salt
- 1 13-ounce can evaporated milk (1⅔ cups)
- 1½ cups milk
- 2 beaten egg yolks
- 1 cup dairy sour cream
- 1 teaspoon vanilla
- 2 egg whites
- ¼ cup sugar
  Whipped cream
  Chocolate curls

Mix first 2 ingredients; add butter. Press firmly over bottom of 9x9x2-inch baking pan. Combine ¾ cup sugar, cocoa, gelatin, coffee, and salt. Stir in milks; beat in yolks. Cook and stir over medium heat till all dissolves and mixture thickens slightly; remove from heat. Slowly stir into sour cream; add vanilla. Chill till mixture mounds. Beat whites to soft peaks; gradually add ¼ cup sugar; beat to stiff peaks. Fold into gelatin mixture. Pour over crust. Chill until mixture is firm. Garnish with whipped cream and chocolate curls. Serves 12.

Looking for a special treat for Easter dinner? Try *Cranberry-Glazed Ham* with a cranberry-wine glaze and sauce. Complement the ham with a garnish of sugary *Frosted Grapes* (see page 73 for the recipe).

Cranberry-Glazed Ham

    1 10- to 14-pound bone-in fully cooked
        ham
      Whole cloves
    1 16-ounce can whole cranberry sauce
    1 cup packed brown sugar
    ½ cup Burgundy
    2 teaspoons prepared mustard

Place ham, fat side up, in shallow roasting pan. Score fat in diamond pattern; stud with cloves. Insert meat thermometer. Bake at 325° till thermometer registers 135° to 140°, 2½ to 3 hours.

In saucepan combine cranberry sauce, sugar, Burgundy, and mustard; simmer, uncovered, 5 minutes. During last 30 minutes baking time, spoon *half* of glaze over ham. Serve remaining with ham. Serves 12.

Parslied Sweet Potatoes

    3 pounds sweet potatoes *or* three
        17-ounce cans sweet potatoes
    6 tablespoons butter or margarine
    ⅓ cup orange juice
    ⅓ cup snipped parsley
    2 tablespoons packed brown sugar

Cook fresh potatoes in boiling salted water till just tender, 30 to 40 minutes. Drain; peel. Cut cooked or canned potatoes crosswise into ½-inch slices. Arrange in 13x9x2-inch baking dish. Sprinkle with salt. Mix butter, orange juice, parsley, and brown sugar; cook and stir over medium heat till butter melts and sugar dissolves. Pour over potatoes; coat well. Cover; bake at 325° till heated through, about 30 minutes. Garnish with orange slices, if desired. Serves 12.

St. Patrick's Day Feast

Serves 8

Blarney Cheese Ball
Assorted Crackers
Glazed Corned Beef
Scalloped Potatoes
Buttered Brussels Sprouts
Tossed Vegetable Salad
Green Goddess Salad Dressing
Hard-Crusted Bread   Butter
Jade Cream Mold
Coffee

BUFFET SERVING TIP: Salute the Irish with a dinner based on the traditional foods and decorating theme of the holiday. Use a green background for the buffet table and a miniature basket of Irish potatoes studded with greenery for a centerpiece. Add shamrocks, pipes, pigs, and bowlers to the scene, either as party favors or as paper cutouts.

Scalloped Potatoes

Canned soup makes a quick and easy sauce—

**8 medium potatoes, peeled and thinly
    sliced (about 8 cups)
¼ cup chopped green pepper
¼ cup minced onion**

**1 10¾-ounce can condensed cream of
    mushroom soup
1 cup milk
2 teaspoons salt
    Dash pepper**

In greased 11x7½x1½-inch baking dish or 2-quart casserole, alternate layers of sliced potatoes, chopped green pepper, and minced onion. Combine condensed cream of mushroom soup, milk, salt, and pepper; pour soup mixture over potatoes in baking dish. Cover; bake at 350° for 45 minutes. Uncover and bake till potatoes are tender, 20 to 30 minutes longer. Makes 8 servings.

Blarney Cheese Ball

**1 8-ounce package cream cheese,
    softened
½ cup dairy sour cream
¼ cup butter or margarine, softened
1 tablespoon snipped parsley
1 teaspoon steak sauce
⅓ cup finely chopped toasted almonds
⅓ cup snipped parsley
    Assorted crackers**

Mix first 3 ingredients; beat till fluffy. Stir in 1 tablespoon parsley and the steak sauce. Chill. Shape into a ball; coat with nuts and ⅓ cup parsley. Serve with crackers.

Glazed Corned Beef

Rinse one 4-pound piece corned beef brisket in cold water to remove pickling juices. Place meat, fat side up, on a rack in a shallow roasting pan. Add 2 cups water; cover pan tightly with foil. Roast at 325° till fork tender, allowing 1 hour per pound. Remove foil carefully and drain liquid from pan; discard. Return corned beef to rack in the shallow roasting pan. Score surface of meat; sprinkle brown sugar over top. Heat at 350° just till brown sugar melts and forms a glaze on top. Carve corned beef across the grain in thin slices. Makes 8 servings.
Note: You can cook meat ahead; wrap and refrigerate. Glaze before serving as above.

Jade Cream Mold

**1 2-ounce package dessert topping mix
1 quart vanilla ice cream, softened
1 pint lime sherbet, softened
¼ cup green crème de menthe
    Chocolate curls**

Prepare topping mix according to package directions. Stir together ice cream, sherbet, crème de menthe, and whipped topping till blended. Turn mixture into one 6-cup mold or two 3-cup refrigerator trays. Freeze. Before serving, unmold dessert and garnish with chocolate curls. Makes 8 servings.

Fourth of July Celebration
Serves 14

Beef-Macaroni Combo
Baked Bean Quintet
Crisp Relish Platter
Vanilla Ice Cream
Devil's Food Cake
Lemonade   Beer

BUFFET SERVING TIP: Set a red, white, and blue buffet with candles, toy soldiers, flags, and drums. Choose napkins and favors that reflect the holiday spirit as well as the color scheme. For background music, select a variety of patriotic songs and marches.

Beef-Macaroni Combo

Remember this casserole for a church supper—

- 4 beaten eggs
- 1 cup catsup
- ⅔ cup milk
- 2 tablespoons instant minced onion
- 2 teaspoons salt
- 2 pounds ground beef
- 2 14-ounce packages macaroni and cheese dinner mix
- ⅔ cup chopped green pepper
- 4 teaspoons prepared mustard
- 1 cup garlic croutons

In large bowl combine beaten eggs, catsup, milk, instant minced onion, and salt. Add ground beef; mix well. Set aside.

Cook macaroni from dinner mixes according to package directions; drain. Stir in green pepper, prepared mustard, and *one* of the cheese sauce packages from dinner mixes.

Spoon macaroni mixture into two greased 12x7½x2-inch baking dishes. Spread *half* meat mixture atop the macaroni in each dish. Sprinkle *half* of the remaining cheese sauce package and *half* of the croutons atop each casserole. Bake, uncovered, at 350° for 35 to 40 minutes. Serves 12 to 16.

Baked Bean Quintet

- 6 slices bacon
- 1 cup chopped onion
- 1 clove garlic, minced
- 1 16-ounce can lima beans, drained
- 1 16-ounce can butter beans, drained
- 1 16-ounce can red kidney beans, drained
- 1 15-ounce can garbanzo beans, drained
- 1 14-ounce jar *or* 16-ounce can baked beans in molasses sauce
- ¾ cup catsup
- ¼ cup packed brown sugar
- ½ teaspoon dry mustard

Cook bacon till crisp; remove and crumble. In pan drippings cook onion and garlic till tender. In 3-quart casserole mix all ingredients and ¼ teaspoon pepper. Bake, covered, at 350° for 1 to 1¼ hours. Serves 14.

Devil's Food Cake

Sift 2¼ cups sifted cake flour; 1¾ cups sugar; and 1 teaspoon *each* salt, baking soda, and baking powder into mixing bowl. Add 1 cup milk and ⅔ cup shortening. Mix till moistened. Beat 2 minutes at medium speed of electric mixer. Add ¼ cup milk; 3 eggs; three 1-ounce squares unsweetened chocolate, melted and cooled; and 1 teaspoon red food coloring. Beat 2 minutes. Bake in 2 greased and lightly floured 9x1½-inch round baking pans at 350° for 30 to 35 minutes. Cool 10 minutes. Remove from pans; cool. Ice with Fudge Frosting.

Fudge Frosting

Butter sides of heavy 3-quart saucepan. In it mix 3 cups sugar, 1 cup milk, two 1-ounce squares unsweetened chocolate, 3 tablespoons light corn syrup, and ¼ teaspoon salt. Cook and stir over low heat till sugar dissolves and chocolate melts. Cook to soft-ball stage (234° on candy thermometer) *without stirring*. Remove from heat; add ¼ cup butter. Cool to warm (110°) *without stirring*. Add 1 teaspoon vanilla; beat till spreadable.

Christmas Buffet

Serves 8

Giblet-Stuffed Turkey
Mashed Potatoes   Gravy
Green Bean Buffet Bake
Della Robbia Wreath Salad
Cranberry Relish
Homemade Rolls   Butter
Apricot Brandy Cake
Milk   Coffee

BUFFET SERVING TIP: Emphasize the Christmas theme of the buffet by dressing the table in festive holiday colors. And design a centerpiece with holly, evergreen branches, pinecones, colorful balls, and an assortment of candles.

Giblet-Stuffed Turkey

    Turkey giblets
  1 cup shredded carrot
  1 cup chopped celery
  ⅓ cup chopped onion
  ½ cup butter or margarine
  7 cups dry bread cubes (about 10 slices bread)
  2 teaspoons ground sage
  ½ teaspoon salt
  ¼ teaspoon pepper
  1 10- to 14-pound turkey

In small saucepan cook giblets in lightly salted water to cover till tender, about 1 hour. Drain giblets; reserve ½ cup cooking liquid. Chop giblets. Cook carrot, celery, and onion in butter till tender. Combine with bread cubes, sage, salt, pepper, and giblets. Toss with reserved liquid; stuff neck and body cavities of turkey. Push drumsticks under band of skin at tail, or tie to tail. Place in shallow roasting pan. Roast at 325° till meat thermometer registers 185°, 4½ to 5½ hours. Remove from oven; let turkey stand for 15 minutes before carving.

Green Bean Buffet Bake

  3 9-ounce packages frozen French-style green beans
  ¼ cup butter or margarine
  2 tablespoons all-purpose flour
  2 teaspoons instant minced onion
  1½ teaspoons salt
  ⅛ teaspoon pepper
  2 cups milk
  ¼ cup grated Parmesan cheese
  1 teaspoon Worcestershire sauce
  1 5-ounce can water chestnuts, drained and sliced
  1 cup soft bread crumbs
  ¼ cup slivered almonds
  1 tablespoon butter or margarine, melted

Cook green beans in a small amount of boiling salted water just till tender; drain well. In a saucepan melt ¼ cup butter or margarine; stir in flour, instant minced onion, salt, and pepper. Add milk all at once. Cook and stir over medium heat till thick and bubbly; remove from heat. Stir in Parmesan cheese and Worcestershire sauce. Add green beans and sliced water chestnuts; mix well. Turn mixture into 1½-quart casserole. Combine bread crumbs, slivered almonds, and the 1 tablespoon melted butter or margarine. Sprinkle crumb mixture over casserole. Bake, uncovered, at 325° till hot through, 50 to 60 minutes. Makes 8 servings.

Cranberry Relish

  ½ cup raisins
  1 pound fresh cranberries
  1½ cups sugar
  2 oranges
  1 grapefruit

In saucepan cover raisins with water; bring to a boil. Remove from heat; let stand 5 minutes. Drain. Put cranberries through food grinder, using coarse blade. Stir in sugar. Peel, section, and dice oranges and grapefruit; stir into cranberries with raisins. Chill overnight; stir occasionally till sugar dissolves. Makes 3 cups.

Della Robbia Wreath Salad

>   1 29-ounce can peach halves (8 halves)
>   1 29-ounce can pear halves (8 halves)
>   1 15¼-ounce can pineapple slices
>   (juice pack)
>   1 17-ounce can peeled whole apricots
>   1 8-ounce package cream cheese,
>   softened
>   8 red maraschino cherries
>   Curly endive
>   Pineapple Dressing
>   Frosted Grapes

Drain canned fruits; chill. Thoroughly dry peaches and pears on paper toweling. Fill peach and pear hollows with *half* of one 8-ounce package cream cheese. Put a cherry in center of *half* the cheese-filled fruit halves; press peach halves together; repeat with pears. Pipe remaining cheese from package through pastry tube to seal halves together.

To serve, arrange bed of curly endive on large platter. Place Pineapple Dressing in bowl in center of platter. Arrange all fruit and Frosted Grapes around dressing. Cover platter loosely and chill till serving time.

Pineapple Dressing

In small saucepan combine ⅓ cup sugar, 4 teaspoons cornstarch, and ¼ teaspoon salt. Gradually blend in 1 cup unsweetened pineapple juice, ¼ cup orange juice, and 2 tablespoons lemon juice. Cook and stir over medium heat till thickened and bubbly. Blend moderate amount of the hot mixture into 2 beaten eggs. Return the mixture to saucepan and cook over low heat 1 to 2 minutes more. Remove mixture from the heat. Gradually stir hot mixture into two 3-ounce packages cream cheese, softened. Chill thoroughly before serving. Makes about 2¼ cups.

Frosted Grapes

Divide 1½ pounds red and green grapes into clusters. Dip clusters into 2 slightly beaten egg whites. Drain. Dip grapes in½ cup sugar. Place on rack to dry for 2 hours.

Apricot Brandy Cake

In large mixing bowl combine 1 package 2-layer-size yellow cake mix, one 2-ounce package dessert topping mix, 4 eggs, and 1 cup cold water; blend till moistened. Beat at medium speed of electric mixer 4 minutes. Pour into greased and floured 10-inch tube pan or 10-inch fluted tube pan. Bake at 350° till done, 45 to 50 minutes. Cool 10 minutes; remove from pan. Place on rack over foil. Prick warm cake many times from top to bottom with long skewer or wooden pick. Slowly spoon Syrup over; repeat with excess Syrup from foil. Let cake stand 3 hours or overnight. Spoon Apricot Glaze over cake; repeat with excess glaze from foil.

Syrup: In small saucepan bring 1 cup sugar and 1 cup water to a boil. Reduce heat; simmer for 1 minute. Remove from heat; stir in ½ cup apricot brandy.

Apricot Glaze: Combine one 12-ounce jar apricot jam (1 cup), sieved, and ¼ cup sugar. Bring to a boil; remove from heat. Stir in 2 tablespoons apricot brandy.

Della Robbia Wreath Salad, named for the lovely ornamental wreaths of the fifteenth century, makes a handsome addition to the buffet table.

New Year's Eve Buffet

Serves 12

Cocktails
Shrimp Cocktail Dip
Caviar Log   Melba Toast Rounds
Rolled Rib Roast
Toasted Barley Bake
Deluxe Peas
Cranberry-Grape Salad
or
Orange-Apricot Ring
Hot Rolls   Butter
Gateau Almond
Coffee

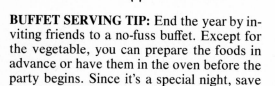

BUFFET SERVING TIP: End the year by inviting friends to a no-fuss buffet. Except for the vegetable, you can prepare the foods in advance or have them in the oven before the party begins. Since it's a special night, save the dessert for the bewitching hour.

Orange-Apricot Ring

  2 16-ounce cans unpeeled apricot halves
  2 3-ounce packages orange-flavored
     gelatin
   Dash salt
  1 6-ounce can frozen orange juice
     concentrate
  2 tablespoons lemon juice
  1 10-ounce bottle lemon-lime carbonated
     beverage, chilled (about 1¼ cups)

Drain apricot halves, reserving 1¼ cups syrup. Puree apricots in sieve or blender. In saucepan heat reserved syrup to boiling; remove from heat. Dissolve orange-flavored gelatin and salt in hot syrup. Add apricot purée, frozen orange juice concentrate, and lemon juice; stir till the concentrate is melted. Slowly pour carbonated beverage down side of pan; mix gently. Pour gelatin mixture into 6½-cup ring mold. Chill till firm. Unmold. Makes 12 servings.

Shrimp Cocktail Dip

  1 8-ounce package cream cheese, cut in
     cubes and softened
  1 cup chili sauce
 1½ tablespoons lemon juice
  1 tablespoon prepared horseradish
  2 teaspoons Worcestershire sauce
  ½ teaspoon salt
    Shelled cooked shrimp, chilled

Put all ingredients *except* shrimp in blender container. Adjust lid; blend till smooth. (When necessary, stop blender and use rubber spatula to scrape down sides.) Pour mixture into small bowl; chill thoroughly. Serve with shrimp. Makes about 2 cups.

Caviar Log

  4 3-ounce packages cream cheese
  1 4¾-ounce can liver spread
  1 2-ounce jar black caviar
    Melba toast rounds

Have cream cheese, liver spread, and caviar at room temperature. Place cheese on waxed paper. Use the paper to pat and shape cheese into a log. Frost evenly with liver spread, then carefully cover log with caviar. Lightly cover with clear plastic wrap; chill at least 1 hour. Serve with melba toast. Makes 1 log.

Cranberry-Grape Salad

  4 cups fresh cranberries
 1½ cups sugar
  2 cups seeded, halved red grapes
  ½ cup broken walnuts
  4 cups tiny marshmallows
  1 cup whipping cream

Grind cranberries through food chopper, using coarse blade. Stir in sugar. Cover and chill overnight. Drain, pressing lightly to remove excess juice. Add grapes, walnuts, and marshmallows to *well-drained* cranberry mixture. Just before serving, whip cream; fold into cranberry mixture. If desired, garnish with grape clusters. Serves 12 to 16.

Rolled Rib Roast

Place one 5-pound boneless beef rib roast, fat side up, on rack in shallow roasting pan. Season with salt and pepper. Insert meat thermometer. Roast, uncovered, at 325° till meat thermometer registers 140° for rare, 160° for medium, or 170° for well-done. Allow about 2¾ hours for rare, about 3¼ hours for medium, and about 4 hours for well-done. Let stand 10 to 20 minutes before carving. Makes 12 servings.

Toasted Barley Bake

   1½ cups quick-cooking barley
   ½ cup finely chopped onion
   ½ cup butter or margarine
   5 cups boiling water
   2 chicken bouillon cubes
   1 teaspoon salt
   2 tablespoons snipped parsley

In skillet cook barley and finely chopped onion in butter or margarine over low heat, stirring frequently, till onion is tender and barley is golden brown. Stir in boiling water, chicken bouillon cubes, and salt. Pour into 2-quart casserole. Bake, uncovered, at 325° till barley is tender, about 1¼ hours; stir mixture once or twice. Stir in snipped parsley. Makes 12 servings.

Deluxe Peas

   3 10-ounce packages frozen peas
   1 cup chopped onion
   ¼ cup butter or margarine
   1 6-ounce can sliced mushrooms, drained
   ¼ cup chopped canned pimiento
   1 tablespoon sugar
   1 teaspoon salt
   ⅛ teaspoon pepper

Cook peas according to package directions; drain. Cook chopped onion in butter or margarine till tender but not brown. Add cooked peas, sliced mushrooms, and chopped pimiento. Stir in sugar, salt, and pepper. Cover and heat through. Makes 12 servings.

Gateau Almond

   ½ cup unsalted butter
   6 slightly beaten eggs
   1 cup sugar
   1 cup all-purpose flour
   ½ teaspoon vanilla
   ½ teaspoon almond extract
       • • •
   Apricot Glaze
   Coffee Buttercream
   Snipped candied apricots

Melt butter; set aside to cool. In bowl combine eggs and sugar; stir till just combined. Set bowl over large saucepan containing 2 inches hot, not boiling water. Heat over low heat, stirring occasionally, till lukewarm, 8 to 10 minutes. Remove from heat. Beat at high speed of electric mixer till light and tripled in volume, about 15 minutes. Gently fold in flour, one-third at a time. Gradually fold in butter, vanilla, and almond extract. Pour into 2 greased and floured 9x1½-inch round baking pans. Bake at 350° till done, 25 to 30 minutes. Cool in pans 10 minutes; remove and cool completely.

To assemble cake, place one cake layer on piece of well-buttered waxed paper. Pour on hot Apricot Glaze; transfer to cake platter. Place second cake layer atop first. Frost with Coffee Buttercream. Chill. If desired, pipe extra Coffee Buttercream through pastry tube over top of cake; garnish with candied apricots. Makes 12 servings.

Apricot Glaze: In small saucepan combine ½ cup sieved apricot preserves and 1 tablespoon brandy; heat mixture to boiling.

Coffee Buttercream: Beat 4 egg yolks till thick and lemon-colored; set aside. Cream 1 cup softened unsalted butter till fluffy; set aside. Combine ⅔ cup sugar, ¼ cup water, and 1 tablespoon instant coffee powder; bring to a boil, stirring to dissolve. Cook over medium-low heat, without stirring, to soft-ball stage (236° on candy thermometer). Quickly pour hot syrup in steady stream into egg yolks beating constantly at high speed of electric mixer. Continue beating till thick and smooth; cool. Beat in butter, a tablespoon at a time. Cover; chill mixture till firm enough to spread, about 30 minutes.

Buffets for Families On the Go

Has mealtime become a monotonous routine for your family? Do work and school schedules often prevent the family from eating together? If so, overcome these problems by serving buffets. Whether the buffet is based in the kitchen or in the family room, the change is fun for all. And, those who must eat and run can do so with a minimum of interruption to others.

To help in organizing your family menus, page through this next section for breakfast, lunch, and dinner buffets—all planned with the busy family in mind. Also note the serving tips included with each menu.

Since family size varies, you'll find a notation on those menus that are quick and easy to double or halve.

A change of locale sparks this delicious Family Room Buffet (see page 102). The menu arranged on a coffee table features *Chicken-Potato Bake, Cucumber-Grape Mold, Sweet Herbed Tomatoes,* and *Easy Cherry Parfaits.*

Breakfasts for Early and Late Risers

Weekend Breakfast

Serves 6

Melon Wake-Up
Canadian-Style Bacon
Graham Cracker Waffles
or
Pumpkin-Nut Waffles
Cinnamon-Apple Topper
or
Butter   Maple Syrup
Milk   Coffee

BUFFET SERVING TIP: Since waffles are a cook-to-order project, they are great for a weekend breakfast buffet. Not everyone is on deck at once, so the meal can be as hurry-up or leisurely as individuals choose. Arrange dishes on the kitchen counter the night before. Prepare and refrigerate the Melon Wake-Up then too. Breakfasters can enjoy the chilled fruit while the waffles bake.

Melon Wake-Up

Set out a small bowl of powdered sugar for those who prefer more sweetness—

    2½ cups strawberries, halved
    3 tablespoons granulated sugar
    1½ cups honeydew melon balls
    1 tablespoon lime juice
        • • •
        Powdered sugar (optional)

Place strawberries in bowl; sprinkle with granulated sugar. Arrange honeydew balls atop strawberries; sprinkle fruit with lime juice. Cover and chill thoroughly.

Before serving, gently toss strawberries with honeydew; sprinkle with powdered sugar, if desired. Makes 6 servings.

Graham Cracker Waffles

You can store this batter in the refrigerator a few hours. Stir before pouring into baker—

    3½ cups all-purpose flour
    1 cup finely crushed graham crackers
        (14 crackers)
    3 tablespoons sugar
    3 tablespoons baking powder
    1½ teaspoons salt
    4 beaten eggs
    4½ cups milk
    1 cup cooking oil
        Cinnamon-Apple Topper
        Shredded sharp American cheese

In mixing bowl thoroughly stir together flour, graham cracker crumbs, sugar, baking powder, and salt. Combine beaten eggs, milk, and cooking oil. Add liquid mixture all at once to dry ingredients; stir only till dry ingredients are moistened. (Makes 8 cups batter.) Bake in preheated waffle baker.

To serve, spoon warm Cinnamon-Apple Topper over each waffle; sprinkle with a little shredded cheese. Serves 6 to 8.

Cinnamon-Apple Topper

A quick waffle topper made with canned apples—

    ½ cup packed brown sugar
    2 tablespoons cornstarch
    ½ teaspoon ground cinnamon
    ¼ teaspoon salt
    1½ cups apple juice
    1 20-ounce can pie-sliced apples
    2 tablespoons butter or margarine
    1 tablespoon lemon juice

In saucepan combine brown sugar, cornstarch, cinnamon, and salt; gradually stir in apple juice. Cook, stirring constantly, till mixture thickens and bubbles. Add apple slices, butter or margarine, and lemon juice; simmer 2 to 3 minutes longer. Serve warm over Graham Cracker Waffles. Makes 4 cups.

The makings of a do-it-yourself breakfast—*Melon Wake-Up, Canadian-Style Bacon,* and the batter for *Graham Cracker Waffles*—wait in the refrigerator while *Cinnamon-Apple Topper* keeps warm on the range.

Pumpkin-Nut Waffles

   2 cups all-purpose flour
   1 tablespoon baking powder
  ¾ teaspoon pumpkin pie spice
   3 beaten egg yolks
1¾ cups milk
  ½ cup cooking oil
  ½ cup canned pumpkin
   3 stiffly beaten egg whites
  ½ cup chopped pecans
    Butter or margarine
    Maple Syrup

Thoroughly stir together first 3 ingredients and ¼ teaspoon salt. Mix yolks, milk, oil, and pumpkin. Stir into dry mixture. Fold in egg whites. Add nuts. (Makes 6 cups batter.) Bake in preheated waffle baker. Serve with butter and Maple Syrup. Serves 6.

Maple Syrup

1 cup light corn syrup
½ cup packed brown sugar
½ cup water
1 tablespoon butter or margarine
  Dash maple flavoring

In saucepan combine corn syrup, brown sugar, and water. Cook and stir till sugar dissolves. Stir in butter and maple flavoring. Makes about 2 cups syrup.

Canadian-Style Bacon

Slash edges of ¼-inch-thick Canadian-style bacon slices. Preheat skillet; brush lightly with cooking oil. Brown the bacon slices quickly, 2 to 3 minutes per side.

Family Brunch

Serves 6 (double for 12)

Orange Nog or Orange Jupiter
Crispy Oatmeal Slices   Sausage
or
Potato-Bacon-Egg Scramble
Buttered Toast   Jelly
Milk   Coffee

BUFFET SERVING TIP: Put your timesaving small kitchen appliances to good use at a breakfast buffet. Let family members help themselves to juice from the blender, fried cereal slices from the grill or eggs from the electric skillet, toast from the toaster, and coffee from the electric pot.

Potato-Bacon-Egg Scramble

    6 slices bacon, cut in 1-inch pieces
    1 5½-ounce package dry hash brown
       potatoes with onion
 1¾ cups water
    ½ teaspoon salt
    6 slightly beaten eggs
    ⅓ cup water
    ½ teaspoon salt
    ⅛ teaspoon pepper
    ½ cup shredded Cheddar cheese
       (2 ounces)

In 10-inch skillet cook bacon till crisp; drain on paper toweling, reserving ¼ cup bacon drippings in skillet. Add hash brown potatoes with onion, 1¾ cups water, and ½ teaspoon salt. Cook, uncovered, over medium heat till liquid is absorbed and bottom begins to brown. Turn potatoes.

Meanwhile, combine eggs, ⅓ cup water, ½ teaspoon salt, and pepper. Pour over potatoes. Cook over low heat, lifting and turning till eggs are done. Sprinkle with shredded cheese and bacon pieces. Makes 6 servings. *To serve 12:* Double the recipe, but use 2 skillets or cook mixture in two batches.

Orange Nog

    ½ cup water
    ½ of a 6-ounce can frozen orange juice
       concentrate (⅓ cup)
    1 8-ounce carton orange yogurt (1 cup)
    1 medium banana, cut in pieces
    6 ice cubes

Blend first 4 ingredients in blender till smooth. With blender running at lowest speed, add ice cubes one at a time; blend smooth. Serve at once. Makes 2½ cups. *To serve 12:* Double all ingredients, but blend only *half* of the mixture at a time.

Orange Jupiter

    ½ cup milk
    ½ cup water
    ½ of a 6-ounce can frozen orange juice
       concentrate (⅓ cup)
    ½ teaspoon vanilla
    ¼ cup sugar
    5 or 6 ice cubes

Blend first 5 ingredients in blender till smooth. With blender running at lowest speed, add ice cubes one at a time; blend smooth. Serve at once. Makes about 3 cups. *To serve 12:* Double all ingredients, but blend *half* of the mixture at a time.

Crispy Oatmeal Slices

    2 cups quick-cooking rolled oats
 1¼ teaspoons salt
    3 cups boiling water
       Butter or margarine
       Maple syrup

In medium saucepan stir oats and salt into boiling water. Cook 1 minute, stirring occasionally. Cover pan; remove from heat and let stand for 5 minutes. Turn cereal into 7½x3½x2-inch loaf pan. Cool; chill for several hours or overnight. Turn out; cut in ½-inch-thick slices. In skillet brown the slices in butter or margarine over medium heat; turn once. Serve with butter and syrup. Serves 6.

Sunday Starter

Serves 6

Apricot Compote or *Berry Blush*
Butterscotch-Nut Roll
or
Mandarin Coffee Cake
Assorted Cold Cereals
Cream and Sugar
Milk   Coffee

BUFFET SERVING TIP: Use the coffee table in the family room to serve Sunday breakfast so that the family members can enjoy a leisurely brunch as they read the paper or catch up on yesterday's activities.

Mandarin Coffee Cake

    1 11-ounce can mandarin orange sections
    2 cups packaged biscuit mix
    2 tablespoons packed brown sugar
    ½ teaspoon grated orange peel
    1 beaten egg
    ⅓ cup milk
    ½ cup raisins
        • • •
    ¼ cup packaged biscuit mix
    ¼ cup packed brown sugar
    ¼ teaspoon ground cinnamon
    2 tablespoons butter or margarine
    1 8½-ounce can pear halves, drained

Drain oranges; reserve ⅓ cup syrup. Set aside ⅔ cup orange sections. Dice remaining sections. Combine 2 cups biscuit mix, 2 tablespoons brown sugar, and orange peel. Combine egg, milk, and reserved syrup. Add to dry mixture with raisins and diced oranges; stir till moistened. Turn into greased and floured 9x1½-inch round baking pan. Combine ¼ cup biscuit mix, ¼ cup brown sugar, and cinnamon; cut in butter till crumbly. Sprinkle atop cake. Slice pears in thirds; arrange atop cake with reserved oranges. Bake at 400° for 25 minutes.

Apricot Compote

    1 13¼-ounce can pineapple chunks
    1½ cups dried apricots
    1¾ cups water
    ⅓ cup sugar
    1 large banana

Drain pineapple, reserving syrup; set aside. Rinse apricots. In medium saucepan combine dried apricots, reserved pineapple syrup, and water. Cover; bring to a boil. Reduce heat; simmer till apricots are tender, about 20 minutes. Stir in sugar during last 5 minutes of cooking. Remove from heat; stir in pineapple chunks. Chill several hours or overnight. Just before serving, slice banana; add to chilled fruits. Makes 8 servings.

Berry Blush

Peel and section 2 medium oranges over bowl to catch juice. To oranges and juice add one 10-ounce package undrained frozen red raspberries, thawed; one 9-ounce carton frozen unsweetened blueberries, thawed (1½ cups); ¼ cup orange marmalade; and 2 teaspoons lemon juice. Toss gently. Chill thoroughly. Makes 6 servings.

Butterscotch-Nut Roll

    1 package refrigerated crescent rolls
       (8 rolls)
    2 tablespoons butter or margarine,
       softened
    ½ cup butterscotch pieces
    ¼ cup chopped nuts

Unroll crescent dough. Moisten perforations and seal, forming a 12x7-inch rectangle. Spread with butter; sprinkle with butterscotch pieces and nuts. Beginning at narrow end, roll up jelly-roll fashion. Place, seam side down, on greased baking sheet; seal ends. Form into semicircle. Make 5 cuts two-thirds through roll at equal intervals. Turn each section on its side. Bake at 375° till roll is golden brown, 15 to 18 minutes. Makes 6 servings.

Ready-to-Eat Lunches

Dagwood Lunch

Serves 8

Chicken-Noodle Soup
Super Dagwood
Cucumber-Onion Relish
Butter Brickle Sundaes
Milk

BUFFET SERVING TIP: Heat the soup in an electric saucepan connected in the serving area, or set up the buffet on the kitchen counter near the range where the soup will be kept at serving temperature over low heat.

Super Dagwood

> 1 12-inch unsliced loaf dark rye bread
> ¼ cup butter or margarine, softened
> 8 slices boiled ham
> 4 slices provolone cheese (6 ounces)
> ½ cup Thousand Island salad dressing
>   Leaf lettuce
> 1 tomato, thinly sliced
> 7 or 8 slices cooked turkey *or* chicken
> 4 or 5 large slices salami

Cut loaf *lengthwise* into four slices; spread cut surfaces with butter. Place bottom slice on platter; top with ham and cheese. Spread with *about* ⅓ of the Thousand Island dressing. Place second slice bread atop cheese; top with lettuce, tomato, and another ⅓ of the dressing. Add third slice bread; top with turkey, salami slices, and remaining dressing. Add top slice bread.

Add cherry tomatoes and pickles to skewers, if desired. Skewer loaf from top to bottom; slice to serve. (Sandwich may be made ahead, covered with clear plastic wrap or foil, and chilled.) Serves 8.

Cucumber-Onion Relish

Combine 3 cups cold water, ½ cup tarragon vinegar, 1 teaspoon sugar, 1 teaspoon salt, and dash pepper. In shallow dish pour mixture over 2 unpeeled cucumbers, thinly sliced, and 1 onion, thinly sliced and separated into rings. Chill. Drain, reserving 2 tablespoons vinegar mixture. Stir reserved liquid into ½ cup dairy sour cream; toss with vegetables. Makes about 4 cups.

Butter Brickle Sundaes

> 1¼ cups crisp rice cereal
> ½ cup chopped walnuts
> ¼ cup butter or margarine, melted
> 2 pints butter brickle ice cream
>   (brick pack, if available)
>   Butterscotch Topping

Crush cereal slightly; toss with walnuts and butter. Pat *half* the mixture in bottom of greased 8x8x2-inch baking pan. Slice ice cream and arrange to fit over cereal layer. Sprinkle remaining cereal mixture atop; press down lightly. Cover; freeze. Cut into squares; top with Butterscotch Topping. Serves 9.

Butterscotch Topping: In large saucepan combine 1 cup packed brown sugar, ½ cup granulated sugar, ½ cup light corn syrup, and 2 tablespoons water. Stir in 1 cup light cream. Bring to a boil over medium heat; stir often. Cook and stir to 218° on candy thermometer, about 5 minutes. Cool; stir in 1 teaspoon vanilla. Refrigerate extra topping in covered jar. Makes 2 cups.

Bumstead would love it

Super Dagwood headlines a noontime buffet set → on a colorful counter, snack bar, or work island in the kitchen. Serve this meal-in-a-sandwich with big mugs of piping-hot soup.

School Day Lunch

Serves 4

Big Beef Bundles
or
Deviled Grilled Sandwiches
California Salad Toss
Kosher Dill Pickles
Fudge-Pecan Bars
Milk

BUFFET SERVING TIP: When lunch hours of family members do not coincide, keep hot sandwiches hot on a warming tray, or in a 200° oven, covered. Grilled sandwiches stay hot if you turn grill to lowest temperature setting and use the appliance as a warmer.

Fudge-Pecan Bars

1¼ cups all-purpose flour
½ cup packed brown sugar
½ cup butter or margarine, melted
1 10-ounce jar fudge topping
1 3-ounce package cream cheese,
　softened
2 eggs
1 teaspoon vanilla
1 cup quick-cooking rolled oats
1 5¾-ounce package milk chocolate
　pieces *or* one 6-ounce package
　semisweet chocolate pieces (1 cup)
⅓ cup chopped pecans

Combine flour, sugar, and butter till crumbly; reserve ⅔ cup. Press remainder in bottom of 9x9x2-inch baking pan. Bake at 350° for 10 minutes. In mixing bowl combine reserved mixture, fudge topping, cheese, eggs, and vanilla; mix well. Stir in oats. Pour over baked layer. Bake at 350° till firm, 20 to 25 minutes. Remove from oven; immediately sprinkle chocolate pieces over top. Spread chocolate when softened; sprinkle with nuts. Cool; cut into bars. Store in refrigerator. Makes 24 bars.

Big Beef Bundles

1 package refrigerated crescent rolls
　(8 rolls)
1 15-ounce can barbecue sauce with meat
½ cup shredded sharp Cheddar cheese
　(2 ounces)
¼ teaspoon paprika
¼ teaspoon dried basil, crushed
½ cup dairy sour cream

Unroll crescent dough; seal perforations to form 4 rectangles. Over *each* rectangle spread *2 tablespoons* of the barbecue sauce with meat. Sprinkle with *2 tablespoons* cheese. Fold rectangles in half, forming 4-inch squares. Press edges closed with fork. Place on greased baking sheet. Sprinkle with paprika and basil. Bake at 375° till golden brown, 12 to 15 minutes. Heat remaining meat sauce with sour cream; *do not boil.* Serve over bundles. Makes 4 servings.

Deviled Grilled Sandwiches

8 slices white bread
　Mayonnaise or salad dressing
1 2¼-ounce can deviled ham
4 slices sharp American cheese
　(4 ounces)
4 thin slices onion
2 beaten eggs
3 tablespoons dairy sour cream
　Butter or margarine

Spread *4 slices* bread with mayonnaise, then with deviled ham. Top with *1 slice each* cheese and onion. Top with remaining bread. Dip sandwiches in mixture of eggs, sour cream, and dash salt. Brown in butter over medium-low heat till golden on both sides and cheese is melted. Makes 4 sandwiches.

California Salad Toss

Combine 3 cups torn lettuce, 3 cups torn romaine, ¾ cup sliced cauliflowerets, ½ cup halved pimiento-stuffed green olives, and 2 tablespoons sliced green onion. Toss with Italian salad dressing. Serves 4.

Seafood-Potato Chowder, tasty morsels of seafood and vegetables simmered in an herb-seasoned broth, is the mainstay of this 'souper' lunch. Dieters note — it is high in flavor and low in calories.

Slimming Lunch

Serves 8

Seafood-Potato Chowder
Oyster Crackers
Lettuce Wedge
Low-Cal Italian Salad Dressing
Celery Sticks   Radishes
Baked Apple
Milk

BUFFET SERVING TIP: To make food portions appear more generous to the dieters in your family, use moderate-size serving dishes and plates. Also, be sure to include some foods that are low enough in calories so that they can return for seconds.

Seafood-Potato Chowder

1 28-ounce can tomatoes, cut up
1 16-ounce package frozen halibut fillets
1 16-ounce package frozen loose-pack hash brown potatoes
1 10-ounce package frozen peas and carrots
1 7-ounce package frozen shelled shrimp
1 tablespoon instant minced onion
2 teaspoons dried parsley flakes
1 teaspoon dried marjoram, crushed
1½ teaspoons salt
     Grated Parmesan cheese

In Dutch oven bring undrained tomatoes and 2 cups water to a boil; add frozen halibut, vegetables, and shrimp. Stir in next 4 ingredients. Cover; bake at 350° for 2 hours; stir occasionally to break up. Top with cheese. Serves 8. (179 calories/serving.)

Low-Budget Lunch
Serves 6 (double for 12)

Frankfurter-Cheese Bake
Mustard Coleslaw
Choco-Polka Dot Squares
Milk   Coffee

BUFFET SERVING TIP: One way to keep hot and cold foods separated on the same dinner plate is to provide individual bowls or custard cups for the coleslaw. This also will help keep the foods at the proper serving temperature.

Frankfurter-Cheese Bake

  ¾ cup macaroni
  6 frankfurters
  ⅓ cup chopped onion
  ⅓ cup chopped green pepper
  2 tablespoons butter or margarine
  3 tablespoons all-purpose flour
  1 teaspoon Worcestershire sauce
  ¼ teaspoon salt
    Dash pepper
  1 cup milk
  1 12-ounce carton cream-style cottage
    cheese (1½ cups)

Cook macaroni in boiling salted water till tender, 8 minutes; drain well. Cut *4 franks* into thin slices; set aside. Cook onion and green pepper in butter till tender but not brown. Blend in flour, Worcestershire, salt, and pepper; add milk all at once. Cook, stirring constantly, till thick and bubbly. Stir in sliced franks, macaroni, and cottage cheese; mix well. Turn into a 1½-quart casserole. Bake at 350° for 20 minutes; stir once. Slice remaining franks diagonally into thirds. Arrange in cartwheel pattern atop casserole. Bake till hot through, about 15 minutes more. Makes 6 servings.
To serve 12: Double all of the ingredients, but bake in two 1½-quart casseroles.

Mustard Coleslaw
A golden, creamy dressing laces this cabbage toss dotted with cucumber, celery, and carrot—

  3 cups shredded cabbage
  ½ cup shredded unpeeled cucumber
  ½ cup chopped celery
  ¼ cup shredded carrot
    • • •
  ½ cup mayonnaise or salad dressing
  4 teaspoons prepared mustard
  1 tablespoon sugar
  1 tablespoon vinegar
  ¼ teaspoon salt

In medium bowl combine shredded cabbage, cucumber, celery, and carrot; chill. In small bowl combine mayonnaise or salad dressing, mustard, sugar, vinegar, and salt; stir till sugar dissolves. Chill thoroughly. Pour dressing over chilled cabbage mixture; toss. Makes 6 servings.

Choco-Polka Dot Squares
A good dessert that is easy to double. You'll appreciate having extra servings in the freezer—

  1 3¾- or 4-ounce package
    regular chocolate pudding mix
  2 tablespoons sugar
  2 cups milk
  1 teaspoon vanilla
  1 cup tiny marshmallows
  ¼ cup crushed peppermint candy
  ¼ cup chopped walnuts
  1 2-ounce package dessert topping mix

In saucepan combine pudding mix and sugar; add milk. Cook and stir over medium heat till mixture boils. Stir in vanilla. Cover with waxed paper; cool to room temperature. Remove paper. Stir in marshmallows, crushed peppermint candy, and chopped nuts.
    Prepare dessert topping mix according to package directions. Fold into pudding mixture. Turn mixture into an 8x8x2-inch baking pan. Freeze till firm. Cut into squares to serve. Makes 6 to 8 servings.
To serve 12: Use large saucepan to combine ingredients. Freeze in two 8x8x2-inch baking pans or one 13x9x2-inch baking pan.

Pizza Lunch

Serves 6

Mushroom-Cheese Pizza
Tossed Italian Greens
Pineapple Ice Cream
Milk

BUFFET SERVING TIP: Ask the youngsters to help make the pizza. They can set up the buffet serving area, too, so that when the pizza is ready the line will move smoothly.

Mushroom-Cheese Pizza

1 package active dry yeast
¾ cup warm water (110°)
2½ cups packaged biscuit mix
    Cooking oil
½ cup finely chopped onion
1 clove garlic, minced
¼ cup cooking oil
2 6-ounce cans sliced mushrooms
1 6-ounce can tomato paste
2 teaspoons brown sugar
1 teaspoon dried basil, crushed
½ teaspoon dried oregano, crushed
½ cup grated Parmesan cheese
6 ounces mozzarella cheese, cut in
    thin strips

Soften yeast in warm water. Add biscuit mix; beat 2 minutes. Turn onto cloth dusted with biscuit mix; knead till smooth (25 strokes). Divide dough in half; roll each piece to a 12-inch circle. Place circles on greased baking sheets; crimp edges. Brush with oil. Bake at 425° for 6 minutes.

Meanwhile, cook onion and garlic in ¼ cup oil till tender. Stir in undrained mushrooms, tomato paste, sugar, basil, oregano, ½ teaspoon salt, and ¼ teaspoon pepper. Heat through, stirring occasionally. Spread over pizza crusts. Sprinkle pizzas with Parmesan. Bake at 425° for 10 minutes. Top with mozzarella; bake 5 minutes more. Serves 6.

Tossed Italian Greens

You'll have dressing left to use another day—

1 envelope Italian salad dressing
    mix
⅔ cup tarragon vinegar
½ cup salad oil
3 tablespoons water
2 tablespoons finely chopped canned
    pimiento
1 tablespoon sugar

• • •

3 cups torn romaine
3 cups torn lettuce
1 cup thinly sliced unpeeled
    zucchini (about 1 small)
½ cup sliced green pepper (1 small)
½ cup sliced celery

In screw-top jar combine first 6 ingredients; cover. Shake well; chill. In salad bowl combine romaine and remaining ingredients; chill. Before serving, toss salad with enough dressing to coat vegetables. Store remaining dressing in covered jar in refrigerator for use another time. Makes 6 servings.

Pineapple Ice Cream

¾ cup sugar
2 tablespoons all-purpose flour
¼ teaspoon salt
2 cups milk
2 beaten eggs
3 cups finely chopped fresh pineapple
½ cup sugar
2 cups whipping cream
½ cup flaked coconut
1½ teaspoons vanilla

In saucepan combine ¾ cup sugar, flour, and salt; gradually stir in milk. Cook and stir over low heat till thick and bubbly. Stir a small amount of hot mixture into eggs; return all to saucepan. Cook and stir 1 minute more. Chill thoroughly.

Combine fruit and ½ cup sugar; add with remaining ingredients to chilled mixture. Pour into a 1-gallon ice cream freezer container. Freeze according to freezer manufacturer's directions. Makes 1 quart.

Dinners that Serve Themselves

Mexican Dinner

Serves 6

Taco Skillet Burgers
Crisp Greens   Avocado Dressing
Onion Breadsticks   Butter
Orange-Pumpkin Custard
Milk   Coffee

BUFFET SERVING TIP: Surprise your family occasionally by serving these popular foods buffet-style. A bright table runner, pottery, and Mexican decorations add to the fun.

Taco Skillet Burgers

    1 beaten egg
    ¼ cup milk
    ½ cup soft bread crumbs
    ⅓ cup finely chopped onion
    1 envelope taco seasoning mix
    1½ pounds ground beef
    1 11½-ounce can condensed bean with
        bacon soup
    2 medium tomatoes, chopped
    1 cup shredded sharp American cheese
    1½ cups corn chips, broken

Mix first 5 ingredients. Add beef; mix well. Shape into 6 patties. In large lightly greased skillet brown the patties on both sides. Mix soup and ½ cup water; spoon over meat. Cover; cook over low heat, 15 minutes. Top with tomatoes and cheese; heat, covered, 3 minutes. Serve with chips. Serves 6.
To serve 12: Double all ingredients, *except* use ½ cup onion. Overlap the browned patties in 13x9x2-inch baking dish. Top with soup mixture. Bake, uncovered, at 375° for 35 minutes. Top with tomatoes and cheese; heat in oven till cheese melts.

Avocado Dressing

    ¾ cup dairy sour cream
    ¼ cup salad oil
    2 tablespoons water
    1 tablespoon lemon juice
    ¼ teaspoon salt
    ¼ teaspoon chili powder
    1 medium avocado, peeled and cubed
    ¼ cup finely chopped green pepper
    ¼ cup finely chopped onion

In blender container place first 6 ingredients. Add cubed avocado. Cover; blend smooth. Reserve 1 tablespoon of the green pepper; stir remaining green pepper and onion into dressing. Cover; chill 1 to 2 hours. Top with reserved green pepper. Makes about 2 cups.

Orange-Pumpkin Custard

    3 slightly beaten eggs
    1 cup canned pumpkin
    ½ cup sugar
    ½ teaspoon ground cinnamon
    ¼ teaspoon ground allspice
    ¼ teaspoon grated orange peel
    1 13-ounce can evaporated milk

Combine eggs, pumpkin, sugar, cinnamon, allspice, and grated orange peel; slowly stir in milk. Pour into six 6-ounce custard cups; set cups in a shallow pan on oven rack. Pour hot water into pan 1 inch deep. Bake at 325° till knife inserted off-center comes out clean, 45 to 60 minutes. Chill. Top with whipped cream and a sprinkle of ground cinnamon, if desired. Makes 6 servings.

Fiesta at home

Mexican seasoning, cheese, and corn chips combine in *Taco Skillet Burgers*. Salad greens are topped with a creamy *Avocado Dressing*.

Family Room Buffet
Serves 6

Chicken-Potato Bake
Cucumber-Grape Mold
Sweet Herbed Tomatoes
Hot Rolls   Butter and Jelly
Easy Cherry Parfaits
Milk   Coffee

BUFFET SERVING TIP: Move dinner into the family room and serve it buffet-style off the coffee table as shown on page 88. Enlist the youngsters to help you carry the food to and from the table. To save extra trips to the kitchen, set out the dessert and coffee with the rest of the food.

Chicken-Potato Bake

    ½ cup chopped onion
    ¼ cup chopped green pepper
    3 tablespoons butter or margarine
    1 10½-ounce can condensed cream of
        chicken soup
    ¼ cup milk
    ½ cup shredded sharp American
        cheese (2 ounces)
    2½ cups cubed cooked chicken
    1 16-ounce can diced carrots, drained
    1 16-ounce package frozen fried potato
        nuggets

In saucepan cook onion and green pepper in butter or margarine till tender but not brown; blend in cream of chicken soup and milk. Remove from heat; add the ½ cup shredded cheese. Stir till cheese melts. Stir in chicken and carrots.

Pour chicken mixture into 12x7½x2-inch baking dish; arrange frozen fried potato nuggets atop casserole. Bake at 375° about 35 minutes. Sprinkle additional shredded cheese atop casserole, if desired; return casserole to oven just till cheese melts, about 2 minutes more. Makes 6 servings.

Cucumber-Grape Mold

    1 3-ounce package lime-flavored gelatin
    1 tablespoon lemon juice
    1 cup lemon-lime carbonated beverage
    1 cup diced, seeded, peeled cucumber
    ½ cup seedless green grapes, halved
        Lettuce

Dissolve gelatin in 1 cup boiling water. Cool to room temperature. Stir in lemon juice. Slowly pour carbonated beverage into gelatin. Stir gently to blend. Chill till partially set. Fold in cucumber and grapes. Pour into 5½-cup mold. Chill firm. Unmold onto lettuce-lined plate. Top with mayonnaise and additional grapes, if desired. Serves 6.

Sweet Herbed Tomatoes

    3 medium tomatoes
    ¼ cup sugar
    ¼ cup salad oil
    ¼ cup vinegar
    1 tablespoon snipped chives
    1 tablespoon snipped parsley
    1 teaspoon dried basil, crushed
    ¼ teaspoon salt
        Dash freshly ground pepper

Peel tomatoes, if desired. Slice into shallow bowl. In screw-top jar combine remaining ingredients. Cover; shake vigorously. Pour over tomatoes. Cover; chill 2 to 3 hours, spooning marinade over tomatoes occasionally. Drain before serving. Makes 6 servings.

Easy Cherry Parfaits

    1 17½-ounce carton frozen vanilla
        pudding, thawed, *or* one 18-ounce
        can vanilla pudding
    1 cup dairy sour cream
    1 21-ounce can cherry pie filling

Combine thawed vanilla pudding and sour cream. In 6 parfait glasses alternate layers of pudding mixture and cherry pie filling, ending with pie filling. Chill the parfaits till serving time. Makes 6 servings.

Low-Calorie Dinner
Serves 8

Saucy Halibut Steaks
Confetti Rice
Cottage-Peach Mold
Honeydew Melon Wedge
Skim Milk   Coffee

BUFFET SERVING TIP: Buffet service is ideal for a family that includes both dieters and non-dieters. While those who can afford seconds are free to replenish their plates at the buffet table, those who are limiting their intake are not tempted by the sight of food remaining on the table.

Cottage-Peach Mold

>   2 envelopes unflavored gelatin
> ½ cup sugar
> ½ teaspoon ground ginger
>   Dash salt
> 1¼ cups water
> 6 or 7 fresh peaches, peeled and pitted
> 2 tablespoons lemon juice
> 1 cup cream-style cottage cheese
>   • • •
>   Lettuce
>   Low-calorie mayonnaise-type salad
>   dressing

In small saucepan combine gelatin, sugar, ginger, and salt; add water. Stir over low heat till gelatin is dissolved. Remove from heat. Puree enough peaches to make 2 cups. Stir into gelatin mixture; add lemon juice. Chill gelatin till partially set.

Chop enough of the remaining peaches to make 1 cup. Fold into gelatin mixture with cottage cheese. Turn into 5-cup mold; chill 5 to 6 hours or overnight.

Unmold on lettuce. Serve with low-calorie mayonnaise-type dressing. Garnish with additional peach slices, if desired. Makes 8 servings. (114 calories/serving.)

Saucy Halibut Steaks

> 4 fresh or frozen halibit steaks
>   (about 1½ pounds)
> 1 beaten egg
> 1 10½-ounce can condensed cream of
>   celery soup
> ¼ cup skim milk
> ¼ cup grated Parmesan cheese
> 3 tablespoons fine dry bread crumbs
> 1 tablespoon butter or margarine,
>   melted

Thaw frozen fish. Place halibut in 11x7½x1½-inch baking pan. In saucepan combine beaten egg, soup, milk, and *half* of the Parmesan cheese. Stir over low heat till cheese melts and mixture is hot. Pour sauce over fish.

Toss bread crumbs with melted butter and remaining Parmesan cheese. Sprinkle atop steaks. Bake at 375° till fish flakes easily when tested with a fork, 20 to 25 minutes. Makes 8 servings. (181 calories/serving.)

Confetti Rice

> 1 cup long grain rice
> 2 cups cold water
> 1 teaspoon salt
> ½ of a 10-ounce package frozen peas
>   (¾ cup)
> ½ cup chopped onion
> ¼ cup slivered almonds
> ¼ cup butter or margarine
> 8 cherry tomatoes, quartered
> ¼ teaspoon seasoned salt
>   Dash pepper

In 2-quart saucepan combine long grain rice, cold water, and 1 teaspoon salt; cover. Bring mixture to boiling; reduce heat to low and continue cooking for 14 minutes. Do not lift cover. Remove rice from heat; let saucepan stand, covered, 10 minutes.

Meanwhile, prepare peas according to package directions. Cook onion and almonds in butter till onions are tender and almonds are lightly browned. Add hot cooked peas, onion mixture, tomatoes, seasoned salt, and pepper to hot rice; toss gently. Keep warm. Makes 8 servings. (168 calories/serving.)

Birthday Buffet

Serves 6

Pork Chop-Stuffing Bake
Twice-Baked Yams
Spiced Apple-Orange Mold
or
Creamy Lime Mold
Cottage-Wheat Rolls   Butter
Ice Cream   Birthday Cake
Milk   Coffee

BUFFET SERVING TIP: Most children enjoy the help-yourself aspects of a buffet. They'll enjoy the meal even more if they don't have to juggle the filled plates on their laps. A conveniently placed card table or individual TV trays solve the problem nicely.

Cottage-Wheat Rolls

3¾ to 4 cups whole wheat flour
2 packages active dry yeast
½ teaspoon baking soda
1 12-ounce carton cream-style cottage
  cheese (1½ cups)
¼ cup packed brown sugar
2 tablespoons butter or margarine
2 eggs

Stir together *1½ cups* of the flour, yeast, and soda. Heat cheese, sugar, butter, ½ cup water, and 2 teaspoons salt till warm (115° to 120°); stir constantly to melt butter. Add to dry mixture; add eggs. Beat at low speed of electric mixer ½ minute; scrape bowl constantly. Beat 3 minutes at high speed. By hand, stir in enough remaining flour to make a moderately stiff dough. On floured surface knead till smooth, 8 to 10 minutes. Place in greased bowl; turn once. Cover; let rise till nearly double (about 1 hour). Punch down. Shape into 24 rolls. Place in greased muffin pans. Let rise till nearly double. Bake at 375° for 12 to 15 minutes. Makes 24.

Pork Chop-Stuffing Bake

Vegetable, stuffing, and meat all in one dish—

6 pork rib chops, cut ¾ inch thick
3 tablespoons butter or margarine
1 cup chopped celery
½ cup chopped onion
3 cups herb-seasoned stuffing mix
1 slightly beaten egg
1 17-ounce can cream-style corn
1 10-ounce package frozen mixed
  vegetables, thawed
Paprika

Trim fat from chops. In skillet cook trimmings till about 1 tablespoon fat accumulates; discard trimmings. Brown the chops in hot fat; season with salt and pepper. Remove chops from pan. Add butter to drippings in skillet. Add celery and onion; cook till tender but not brown. Remove skillet from heat; add stuffing mix, tossing to coat. Combine egg and corn; blend with stuffing. Spoon mixture into 12x7½x2-inch baking dish; sprinkle with mixed vegetables. Top with browned chops. Bake, covered, at 350° for 55 minutes. Sprinkle the pork chops with paprika. Makes 6 servings.

Twice-Baked Yams

Potatoes and main dish finish together when
you give the potatoes a 20-minute head start—

6 medium yams *or* sweet potatoes
• • •
⅓ cup apricot preserves
¼ cup butter or margarine
1 teaspoon salt
Orange juice
Ground nutmeg

Bake potatoes at 350° till done, 50 to 60 minutes. Cut slice from top of each potato; scoop out inside, being careful not to break shell. In mixing bowl mash potatoes. Add preserves, butter, salt, and enough orange juice (if needed) to moisten; beat with electric mixer or rotary beater till fluffy. Pile lightly into shells; sprinkle with nutmeg. Bake at 350° till hot through, 15 to 20 minutes. Makes 6 servings.

Spiced Apple-Orange Mold

Drain one 11-ounce can mandarin orange sections, reserving syrup. Add water to syrup to make 1½ cups. In saucepan combine syrup mixture, 2 tablespoons vinegar, 1½ inches stick cinnamon, and 3 whole cloves; bring to a boil. Add oranges; simmer, covered, for 10 minutes.

Remove from heat; drain oranges, reserving syrup. Discard spices. Dissolve two 3-ounce packages lemon-flavored gelatin in hot syrup; stir in 2 cups apple juice. Chill till partially set. Fold in oranges and ¾ cup chopped unpeeled apple (1 medium). Pour into 5½-cup mold. Chill firm. Unmold onto lettuce-lined platter. Garnish with additional mandarin orange sections, if desired. Makes 6 to 8 servings.

Creamy Lime Mold

    1 8¾-ounce can crushed pineapple
    1 3-ounce package lime-flavored gelatin
    ½ pint lime sherbet (1 cup)
    1 cup seedless green grapes, halved
    ½ cup chopped celery
    ½ cup whipping cream

Drain pineapple; reserve syrup. Add water to reserved syrup to make 1 cup. In saucepan bring syrup mixture to a boil; remove from heat. Add gelatin; stir to dissolve. Add sherbet, a spoonful at a time; stir to melt. Chill till partially set.

Fold green grapes and celery into partially set mixture. Whip cream; fold into gelatin mixture. Pour into 4½-cup mold. Chill till firm. Makes 6 servings.

Colorful food attractively arranged is one of the great appeals of a buffet meal. The colors and flavors of *Pork Chop-Stuffing Bake*, *Spiced Apple-Orange Mold*, and *Twice-Baked Yams* harmonize well.

Penny-Wise Dinner
Serves 6

Golden Corn Squares
Buttered Zucchini Slices
Bean-Green Toss
Biscuits   Honey Butter
Fruit Cocktail Crisp
Milk   Coffee

BUFFET SERVING TIP: Serving this meal buffet-style needn't require special appliances or warming equipment. Instead, make use of inexpensive wicker baskets, colorful potholders, and wooden wall plaques to set under hot dishes. Use an assortment of trays for carrying food from the buffet to the table; let family members select the size tray that best suits their appetite and dexterity.

Bean-Green Toss
An easy fix-up for canned green beans —

⅓ cup salad oil
¼ cup vinegar
2 teaspoons sugar
½ teaspoon salt
½ teaspoon dry mustard
½ teaspoon dried thyme, crushed
¼ teaspoon paprika
1 16-ounce can cut green beans, drained
⅓ cup chopped celery
6 cups torn lettuce
1 medium tomato, peeled, seeded, and finely chopped

In screw-top jar combine salad oil, vinegar, sugar, salt, dry mustard, thyme, and paprika; cover and shake vigorously. Pour dressing mixture over drained green beans and chopped celery in shallow dish; cover and refrigerate 4 to 6 hours.

Before serving, combine lettuce and tomato in salad bowl. Add bean mixture; toss together lightly. Makes 6 servings.

Golden Corn Squares
A thrifty main dish with flavor —

3 slightly beaten eggs
1 17-ounce can cream-style corn
¼ cup milk
1 tablespoon instant minced onion
⅛ teaspoon pepper
½ cup long grain rice, cooked (1½ cups)
1 12-ounce can luncheon meat, cut in ¾-inch cubes
½ cup cubed American cheese (2 ounces)

Combine eggs, corn, milk, onion, and pepper; stir in rice, meat, and cheese. Turn into an ungreased 10x6x2-inch baking dish. Bake at 350° till a knife inserted just off-center comes out clean, 45 to 50 minutes. Let stand 10 minutes before serving. Cut into squares. Makes 6 servings.

Fruit Cocktail Crisp

1 30-ounce can fruit cocktail
¼ cup granulated sugar
2 tablespoons all-purpose flour
1 tablespoon lemon juice
• • •
⅔ cup all-purpose flour
⅔ cup quick-cooking rolled oats
½ cup packed brown sugar
6 tablespoons margarine or butter, melted
1 2-ounce package dessert topping mix
½ teaspoon ground ginger

Drain fruit; reserve ½ cup syrup. In medium saucepan combine granulated sugar and 2 tablespoons flour; blend in reserved syrup. Cook and stir over medium heat till thick and bubbly. Remove from heat; stir in lemon juice and fruit. Set aside.

Combine ⅔ cup flour, oats, brown sugar, and margarine; pat *half* of mixture in bottom of 10x6x2-inch baking dish. Spoon fruit over; sprinkle with remaining crumb mixture. Bake at 350° for 30 minutes.

Combine topping mix and ginger. Prepare topping according to package directions. Serve over warm dessert. Serves 6 to 8.

Menu Index

Recipe Index

D-G

T-Z